D0434843

In a time when pure biblical manhood is not only rare but often outright outlawed, Craig Groeschel's *Fight* reminds us that God created us to be warriors. If every Christian man really got this message, I believe the world would be changed forever.

—Dave Ramsey,
New York Times bestselling author and
nationally syndicated radio show host

Craig Groeschel's new book *Fight* sends a resounding message to all men that they have what it takes to win the battles they are trying to fight. If you are tired of struggling and want to rediscover the warrior within, this book is for you.

—Mark Burnett,
award-winning executive producer of *The Bible*

Other Books by Craig Groeschel

Altar Ego: Becoming Who God Says You Are

Chazown: A Different Way to See Your Life

*The Christian Atheist: Believing in God
but Living as If He Doesn't Exist*

*Daring to Drop the Pose
(previously titled Confessions of a Pastor)*

God, Love, and Sex (previously titled Going All the Way)

It: How Churches and Leaders Can Get It and Keep It

Soul Detox: Pure Living in a Polluted World

Weird: Because Normal Isn't Working

What Is God Really Like? (general editor)

FIGHT

WINNING THE BATTLES
THAT MATTER MOST

CRAIG GROESCHEL

ZONDERVAN

Fight
Copyright © 2013 by Craig Groeschel

This title is also available as a Zondervan ebook. Visit www.zondervan.com/ebooks.

This title is also available in a Zondervan audio edition. Visit www.zondervan.fm.

Requests for information should be addressed to:
Zondervan, *Grand Rapids, Michigan 49530*

Library of Congress Cataloging-in-Publication Data

Groeschel, Craig.
    Fight : winning the battles that matter most / Craig Groeschel.
      pages cm
    ISBN 978-0-310-33374-6
    1. Christian men — Religious life. I. Title.
  BV4528.2.G753 2013
  248.8'42 — dc23   2013012512

Craig Groeschel is represented by Thomas J. Winters of Winters & King, Inc., Tulsa, Oklahoma.

Cover design: Dual Identity
Cover photo: Alfonse Pagano / Getty Images®
Interior images: Dual Identity
Interior design: Sarah Johnson

Printed in the United States of America

13 14 15 16 17 18 19 20 /DCI/ 22 21 20 19 18 17 16 15 14 13 12 11 10 9 8 7 6 5 4 3 2 1

CONTENTS

FIGHT
LIKE A MAN

It's not the size of the dog in the fight,
it's the size of the fight in the dog.
—*Mark Twain*

1.1

FIGHT LIKE A MAN

I learned how to fight in the second grade. I was walking home from school one day, minding my own second-grader business. Suddenly, a much larger third-grader, Bo Talbot, loomed before me, planting himself squarely in my path. Bo was only one year older than I was, but I was convinced that his parents had kept him out of school for a few years to be molded by UFC trainers, bruisers who gave him steroids to snack on between weightlifting sessions.

Bo grabbed my shirt with one hand, drawing his other hand back into a fist the size of a wrecking ball. Through clenched teeth, he snarled, "Groeschel, are you *gay?*"

Since it was 1975 and I was only eight years old, I wasn't really sure what *gay* meant. As my mind raced to respond, I landed on my mom's one lifelong rule: always tell the truth. Squinting up at him, bracing myself for his fist's meteoric impact, I stammered, "I-I-I'm not sure. C-c-can I get back to you tomorrow?"

Truth can be a dazzling weapon. Bo was startled by my stalling tactic. He stood there for several seconds, frozen like a statue of a Greek warrior, mulling it over. After an awkward silence, he released me and said, "Okay. But you *better* tell me tomorrow." He walked away, and the crisis was temporarily placed on pause.

Whew! Mom was right. Always tell the truth.

Trembling, I scampered home and found my mother piling my dirty socks into the washing machine. My future hanging in the balance, I blurted out my big question, not revealing my near-death experience. As nonchalantly as I could, I asked, "Mom, what does *gay* mean?"

She hesitated — the same way I hesitated recently when my eight-year-old daughter asked me how she got into her mom's tummy before she was born. My mom's hesitation should have raised a red flag for me, but I guess in my heightened state of fear, I overlooked it.

"Honey," she said with calming assurance, "*gay* just means 'happy.'"

And that was the moment my mom broke her own rule and ruined her perfect record.

Huh. So gay means happy. That made sense to my second-grade mind, even if it seemed strange that a bully would ask about my happiness.

The next day after school, I found myself cornered by Bo once again. Like an actor resuming his place onstage, he stood over me, his fist drawn back, using my shirt collar as a handle. Then he asked the fateful question, drawing out the words for dramatic effect: "Craig, are ... you ... gay?"

I grinned broadly, proud to know how to answer. "Sure am. Been gay my whole life. I'm probably the gayest guy you've ever met!"

I don't remember much of what happened after that. I do remember a ringing sound and a metallic flavor in my mouth, the disinctive taste of blood. I understood then why a cartoon character who gets hit sees stars and sometimes little birds. Bo's wallop gave me a vivid glimpse into the cartoon dimension.

The whole side of my face swelled like a melon. My head weighed twice as much as the rest of my body. As my watery eyes came clear, I blinked there in Bo's shadow, his massive frame still towering over me. He promised there would be plenty more beatings, every day after school for the rest of my life. Then he walked away.

At that moment, I didn't feel very gay at all.

When the dizziness wore off enough that I could stand, I staggered home in shame. My very first fight and I didn't even get a punch in. Getting beaten up was bad enough. Getting beaten up for being happy was infinitely worse.

HOLDING OUT FOR A HERO

We love to root for the underdog. We love to see good triumph over evil and courage defeat cowardice. We love to see righteousness prevail and unrighteousness punished. And we love a hero who refuses to give up the fight no matter how impossible the odds.

Right now we're starving for heroes. We're no longer surprised when men we once admired and respected — elected officials, superstar athletes, gifted pastors — tumble in a sex scandal, an embezzlement scheme, or a domestic abuse arrest. We've almost become jaded, half-expecting our leaders and favorite celebrities to be hiding something. Most are, right?

We hope they'll make sacrifices, take risks, and make hard decisions to do the right thing, but we aren't surprised when they don't. We lack real heroes, and Hollywood fills the void with a glut of superheroes — Iron Man and Batman and Thor and Spider-Man and Avengers and X-Men — dazzling us with their powers in 3D and on Blu-ray. But we still long for someone to show us what an authentic flesh-and-blood hero looks like.

Where have all the good men gone?

I read a book recently that suggests that our culture has tried to turn the good men into women — nicer, softer, kinder, more compassionate, and fashion savvy. Forgive me for stating the obvious, but men are not women. (For the record, women don't make good men either.) After all, God created us differently. "So God created human beings in his own image. In the image of God he created them; male and female he created them" (Gen. 1:27 NLT). Both men and women reflect the image of God, but in distinct ways.

Wild at heart

I'm convinced that one of the most profound ways has to do with how we use our manhood. God created men to have the heart of a warrior, placing a desire within us to stand up and fight for what's pure, for what's true. A man has a warrior's heart. You have a warrior's heart. You itch for a fight. That's God's design, not ours. That doesn't mean that men should be aggressive, alpha-bully punks. (Nor does it mean that women can't fight for what's right as well.) It simply means that within every man, God has planted a divine desire to fight for righteousness.

Think about it this way. There are two kinds of movies: chick flicks and, well, everything else. Do chick flicks inspire men? Do they make them want to be stronger, braver, better men? Remember that Cary Grant movie, *An Affair to Remember*? Remember when Deborah Kerr's character says, "If you can paint, I can walk — anything can happen, right?" Have you ever known a guy to *watch* that movie? If you're a guy, you don't even know what I'm talking about, do you?

What about in *Pride and Prejudice* when Keira Knightley's character says to her new husband, "You may only call me 'Mrs. Darcy' when you are completely and perfectly and incandescently happy." And he responds with, "Then how are you this evening ... Mrs. Darcy?" and kisses her on the forehead. And then, "Mrs. Darcy," as he kisses her on the cheek. And then, "Mrs. Darcy," as he kisses her on the nose. Again, if you're a guy, you have no idea what I'm talking about, right? Or if you do know, you're trying hard to forget.

What about *Braveheart*? Mel Gibson, blue-faced, says, "Fight, and you may die. Run, and you'll live. At least a while. And dying in your beds, many years from now, would you be willing to trade *all* the days, from this day to that, for one chance — just one chance — to come back here and tell our enemies that they may take our lives [raising his sword over his head], but they'll never take *our freedom?*"

Remember *Gladiator*? Russell Crowe, in his cool Roman general uniform, spurs his horse forward through the forest, calling, "Brothers, what we do in life echoes in eternity!"

For men, there's a part of us that thinks, *I wish I could have been there. I would have fought.* You don't have to hide it from me. A part of me thinks that too. You know why? Because that's how we're wired. Men are supposed to respond that way. A man with nothing to fight for quickly becomes a frustrated man, often without a clue as to why.

Fighting for what's right stirs something inside a man. It makes him want to be not *just* a man but *the* man. The *best* man he can be. A man knows deep inside himself what God wants him to be: a hero with a warrior's heart.

★ BE THE MAN ★

A few months after my wife, Amy, and I got married, something dawned on her that she hadn't thought of before: she had married *a man*. I do things a lot differently than women do. We'd been married four years when it finally came to a head. We had just gotten our first dishwasher, and one day I foolishly attempted to load it by myself. I *thought* I was helping, but I didn't realize there's a *right* way to load a dishwasher and, apparently, a *wrong* way. I figured, just stuff everything in, start it, and you're good.

When Amy saw my attempt to be helpful, she gasped. "Craig! You loaded it all wrong!"

"Wrong? How could it be *wrong*?" We had a little spat, which ended with her sighing and saying, "Oh, Craig, you're just such a ... *a man!*" I thought, *Uh, hello! Darn right, I'm a man.* For years, scenarios just like this one played out, with her doing things her way and me doing things like a man. Eventually, she'd say, "Couldn't you just do this more like a *woman*?" One day I finally got fed up. "You should have married a woman. I'm *never* gonna be able to do this like a woman."

Then one time when Amy and I were having one of these differences of opinion, it looked like it was going to end like it always did—in a draw. But then my amazing wife said something so profound, it changed my life. "Craig," she said, "I want you to know something. Right now, as of this moment, I am choosing to one hundred percent completely embrace you as the man that God created you to be. I won't ask you to be anything else." From that moment on, our marriage improved like you wouldn't believe.

Let me clarify something here. I'm not saying men are better and they need to lord over women like tyrants. I'm not saying women are better and need to emasculate their husbands. I'm simply saying that we're different, and since it was God who made us this way, that's a good thing. That day, Amy recognized the difference, and she empowered me to embrace the fullness of being God's man for her and for our family. So let me say a couple more things that you need to know as you read along.

Guys, this book is for you. The last thing you need is another book, podcast, motivational CD, or even Bible study that tells you how to be a man of God in four easy steps. That's not what we're doing here. We're focusing on the core issue that I'm convinced will motivate you deep within your heart: being a warrior and knowing when and how to fight.

If you read this book, you will uncover who you really are— a man created with a warrior's heart in the image of God—and how to fight the good fight for what's right. You will find the strength to fight the battles you know you need to fight—the ones that determine the state of your heart, the quality of your marriage, and the spiritual health of your family. The battles that make you dependent on God as the source of your strength. The battles that make you come *alive*.

Ladies, if you're reading this book, you probably should put it down. It's not for you.

Put it down. Please. *Now.*

I'm serious.

You're still reading, aren't you?

I understand, and really I want you to keep reading. Just like I wanted Amy to understand that I can never be anything other than a man, I believe most husbands want their wives to recognize the same about them. So if you're going to keep reading, I hope you will use this as an insider's guide to help your man fight the right battles. And not just to fight them but to win them. I hope you'll empower him to be who God made him to be.

If you do, he will exceed your wildest dreams. He'll blow your old expectations away. So if you're going to keep reading, please don't try to make him into what you think you want. Just encourage him to be the man God created him to be. Simply recognize that God put something different inside him: the heart of a warrior.

//////////////////////////////★//////////////////////////////

WE ARE THE WARRIORS

//////////////////////////////★//////////////////////////////

The Bible says that God is a God of mercy and grace. And in Exodus we're told that "the Lord is a *warrior*; the Lord is his name" (15:3, emphasis mine). So if we're created in God's image, as we saw in Genesis, then we too are warriors as part of our nature. Again, I'm not saying that women can't be warriors too. It's just that being a warrior is core to men's identity. It's not just a cultural, patriarchal thing. It's a God thing, inherent in our Creator's design.

Consider what the Bible has to say about fathers, another term that's used to describe God as well as men. Psalm 127:4–5 says, "Like arrows in the hands of a *warrior* are sons born in one's youth. Blessed is the man whose quiver is full of them. They will not be put to shame when they contend with their enemies in the gate" (NIV 1984, emphasis mine).

Warriors.

And then there's the greatest warrior who ever lived, Jesus. Many of us imagine Christ based on the pictures we've seen painted of him, meek and mild, smiling. Children gathered at his feet adoring him. Sheep flitting about on the hillsides around him. Healing the sick, comforting the poor. Just a gentle force for good wherever he floats.

I'm exaggerating (but only slightly). If you look at the life of Christ, he was not a divine doormat. Imagine Jesus, with righteous anger, violently toppling the tables of the corrupt money changers in his Father's temple. Or consider this picture of Christ's return as envisioned by John: "I saw heaven standing open and there before me was a white horse, whose rider is called Faithful and True. With justice he judges and wages war. His eyes are like blazing fire, and on his head are many crowns.... He is dressed in a robe dipped in blood, and his name is the Word of God.... Coming out of his mouth is a sharp sword with which to strike down the nations. 'He will rule them with an iron scepter.' ... On his robe and on his thigh he has this name written: KING OF KINGS AND LORD OF LORDS" (Rev. 19:11 – 16).

This is the Good Shepherd, meek and mild? If you're like most Christians, you're probably thinking, *That's not how I picture Jesus, as some wild warrior leading with a war cry. Christians aren't supposed to fight back. Whatever happened to turning the other cheek?*

Turning the other cheek comes from Matthew 5:38 – 39, where Jesus teaches, "You have heard that it was said, 'Eye for eye, and tooth for tooth.' But I tell you, do not resist an evil person. If someone slaps you on the right cheek, turn to them the other cheek also."

Certainly Jesus is the promised Prince of Peace (Isa. 9:6). God's mercy and compassion are new every morning (Lam. 3:22 – 23). God has given us so much more than we could ever deserve, sacrificing his own Son for our sins (John 1:29; 3:16; Heb. 10:10).

These and other truths have led many people to imagine Jesus as meek and mild, a poor Galilean carpenter who played with children and tended sheep. The problem with this depiction is not so much that it is inaccurate as that it is incomplete. Such a "snapshot" of Jesus typically comes from just a few Bible verses (sometimes even just one verse). That kind of cherry-picking can give us only part of the whole picture.

We must consider all of what the Bible tells us to fully appreciate God's character and Jesus' example. This is what we'll be doing throughout this book: looking not only at the life of Christ but also at the life of someone who bore some startling similarities to most men today—our good buddy Samson. Yep, the dude with the rippling biceps and hippie hair and a thing for Delilah. You may be surprised by how much we have in common with this guy. Things didn't turn out so well for him in the end, but by looking at his life, we'll learn how to defeat the demons that make strong men weak. We'll learn how to become who God made us to be: men who know how to fight for what's right.

SMACKDOWN ON THE SLAYGROUND

When I stumbled home with Bo's knuckle-prints on my face, my mom was horrified to see my shiner. As bad as that looked, my ego was in far worse shape. She ran to me, scooping me into her arms. "Honey, what happened? Oh, sweetheart, are you okay?"

Choking back tears as she held me, I told her what Bo had done to me. Like many moms, she was appalled by the violence a bully could inflict. When my dad came home a couple of hours later, she recounted the story as I stood next to her, watching his reaction.

He listened silently, standing there in his tie, sizing me up, his mouth scrunched to one side, his hands on his hips, still holding his jacket. Then instead of consoling me as my mother had, he raised my chin, turned me around, placed his big hands firmly on my shoulders, walked me out to the garage, and sat me down on an overturned bucket. Within a matter of minutes, he had transformed our garage into a training facility that Rocky would envy. Once he had everything situated the way he wanted, he returned to me and said simply, "Now I'm gonna teach you to fight. You're gonna find this Bo punk and set things right."

That was it. No hugs. No bandaids. No anger. No blame. No tears. I had a problem, and Dad had a solution: lessons in honest-to-God bare-knuckle brawling. In the most powerful of ways, my father had just shown me how much he loved me.

For the rest of the weekend, he taught me every trick he knew or could invent. He demonstrated how to jab, how to block, and how to unleash a knockout punch. He instructed me in the finer points of throwing elbows, choking, and pushing pressure points. He showed me how to tackle, poke eyes, scratch, bite, and how to kick a guy in the place guaranteed to end the fight.

Dad didn't teach me to fight fair. He taught me to fight to win.

To wrap up my training, Dad gave me instructions on what to say and do to Bo. If Bo cooperated, I shouldn't punch him. But if he refused my terms, I should fire my first punch fast and hard to his nose. As his eyes started to water, I was immediately to snap-kick his groin. This simple combination would allow me to finish the fight however I pleased.

When my mom realized what we were doing, she was furious with Dad. "You're going to get our son hurt. Violence doesn't solve anything." My dad stood his ground, as calm and resolute as an army general. "You have to trust me, honey. Craig *has* to stand up to this bully. He needs to win this fight, and win it decisively. And he will."

On my way to school on Monday, my body was so infused with nervous energy my knees wobbled and I felt dizzy. As I turned the corner into the school playground, there was Bo, about halfway across the field, just standing around with some other boys. Driven by my dad's programming, I walked upright, shoulders back, in a straight line directly to my adversary. I had no idea what was going to happen. I was simply following the script.

Bo happened to turn just in time to meet my face, leaning inches from his own, glaring at him. Before he could even register what was happening, I grabbed his shirt and yanked him toward me, and my right fist cocked like a catapult locked and loaded. It wasn't courage. Just like my dad taught me, I channeled all my righteous indignation and raw fear and blind rage into my tiny arms and hands, fortified by my father's confidence in me.

"If you *ever* touch me again, Bo, I ... will ... *finish* ... what you started. Do you understand me?" It was hard to believe that was actually my voice delivering an ultimatum to the kid who had cleaned my clock only days before.

But in that moment, the sun froze in the sky. Birds stopped flying. The other boys' jaws hung open. Bo quit breathing momentarily as his eyes locked with mine, probing for an accurate read on the situation. *Is he bluffing? Would he really hit me?* The staredown seemed to last for eons, both of us refusing to blink.

Then, just as suddenly as I had grabbed him, Bo laughed and held up his open palms. He leaned back and awkwardly broke the silence: "Uh ... okay, then. I didn't *really* think you were gay anyway."

And just like that, Bo and I became friends. And not only friends but brothers bound by blood. We never talked about it again, and to this day I'm surprised that I could back down a guy who outweighed me by at least twenty pounds. (That's a lot when you weigh only fifty.) But I did.

My dad had empowered me to stand my ground. That one simple gift, offered in love — a few hours of his time, passing knowledge and skill from one man to another — not only changed the boy I was then but even shaped the man that I am today. Even if Bo had knocked me down again, it wouldn't have mattered, because I had stood up to him. I had learned how to fight like a man.

That was the only time in my life that my dad ever encouraged me to fight back. But the grizzled warrior in him reached out to the budding warrior in me with the clear lesson that some wrongs can be made right only when you decide to fight back.

PICK YOUR BATTLES

If all this talk about fighting and violence and being a warrior bothers you, let me just say this: the virtue of strength is determined by how it's used. If it's used to love and to protect, it's good. Unfortunately, it can also be used to inflict harm, and that's not consistent with what we see of God's character in the Bible. He calls us to fight for what's right. And a warrior is only as worthy as his cause.

A man without a cause from God is often just an angry man who doesn't know where to direct his pent-up energy and aggression. A warrior *with* a cause from God directs that warlike energy for a cause greater than himself.

Gentlemen, God created *you* with the heart of a warrior.

Until there's something you're willing to die for, you can't truly live.

You were created to fight for righteousness.

Until you tap into that divine cause, you'll be bored, destructive, and frustrated. Find something more. I thank God I get to live my divine cause. I honestly believe I'm on the front lines of the most important war: the one between heaven and hell. The kingdom of God versus the kingdom of darkness. My sword is drawn, and I'm on the front lines. I'm willing to die for the cause to lead people to become fully devoted followers of Christ. That's not *what I do*; that's *who I am*. It starts with my family, and it bleeds into everything I do anywhere I am.

Recently, I had this very powerful moment with a group of college students who visited the church where I preach. The young gals usually attended another one of our church locations in another community where our messages are broadcast via video, so they had listened to me preach for a couple of years. After the message that day, several girls from this group came up to talk to me. They were very gracious, basically telling me, "Pastor Craig, we're so thankful for you! Our dads didn't set an example for us as godly men. We appreciate what you do. You're such a strong man of God. We pray all the time that we'll find strong men of God like you that we can marry."

I was flattered, and also kind of embarrassed. I laughed and told them, "Wow. Thank you so much. But I feel like you need to understand something: I'm not strong at all. I'm actually one of the weakest men you've ever met."

They looked confused, so I tried to explain. "What you really want is not some guy who looks strong on the outside. You want a man who can stand strong only because he spends time on his knees every day before God."

(Ladies, if you are still reading, don't miss this. The man you want isn't the guy who wins tough-guy fights but the man who knows his weaknesses and fights in God's strength. He won't be perfect. But God will be perfecting him.)

Every guy wants to be strong.

Maybe you'd like to make the cover of *Men's Health* or something, a cocky little half-smile on your face, flexing your massive biceps as you slightly lift your tight V-neck shirt to reveal your ripped abs underneath.

That's what many men *think* they want. But guys who invest their lives only in physical strength don't advance God's kingdom in the world—at least not that way. Men who are strong, men who are world-changers, men who are truly warriors are men who can admit their limitations.

"Lord, I'm weak. And I need you."

I want to redefine the way you think about what it means to be a warrior. It's not about cockiness and attitude; it's not about six-pack abs and picking fights; it's not about succeeding in life and winning everyone's admiration or envy. Being a true warrior is about knowing the source of true strength. It's about knowing your weaknesses and turning to God to empower you to be the man he made you to be. You don't have to become Jason Bourne or James Bond (Sean Connery or Daniel Craig, not those other wimps) to be a warrior.

So if you're a peace-loving dude who feels like he's not really struggling with any major problems, then keep reading. This book is still for you. You're already in a fight, whether you know it or not. Your spiritual enemy wants to take you out. He's a master at making strong men weak. Sometimes he does that by making us comfortable, secure, and safe, resigned to a mediocre life because it's familiar and doesn't require much from us. Is that really how you want to live?

Though Satan makes strong men weak, God is in the business of making weak men strong. Your past isn't the most important thing. Your future is. If you want to live your life—really live it in a bold, passionate, life-giving way that's contagious—then this book is for you. As we'll discover and explore together, God often uses the painful moments we dread the most to do something deep within us. It's how God shapes us to be the men he wants us to be.

If there are no struggles, there is nothing to fight for.

And God has a unique way of awakening the dormant warrior within to fight one battle that prepares us to fight and win an even bigger one.

FIGHT CLUB

Not only does God want you to fight, he wants to give you a cause greater than yourself. Then, once you love something enough that you're willing to die for it, you'll be set free to live. Consider what the leader Joab said to inspire his warriors in 2 Samuel 10:12: "Be strong, and let us fight bravely *for our people and the cities of our God*" (emphasis mine). Fight for a cause greater than yourself. It's in you.

You know it's there.

You can feel it.

You have the heart of a warrior.

Maybe you're thinking, *I don't know, Craig. I'm a laid-back dude, peaceful, live-and-let-live. I'm not really into that whole fight-club scene. Call of Duty's pretty great and all, but actually, I don't even know if I know how to fight and would rather not.*

It's okay if you don't think of yourself as a warrior, at least in earthly terms. But God has made you to fight battles. And he's given us many spiritual weapons, which we'll discuss along the way. But for now, just consider that the strongest man is not the one who lifts the most weight but the one who has the most faith.

Others of you may be thinking, *There really is a battle brewing. And I can't afford to lose it.* If that's you, it's time for you to fight.

Maybe you're in danger of failing financially. Now is the time to fight like your life depends on it, to get control of your budget and align your priorities with your cash flow.

Perhaps you're playing with a lustful fire. You keep returning to images and people and places that excite you but also unleash something you're afraid you can't control. You're going to get burned. Decide. Confess and overcome this darkness.

Fight.

Your marriage might be hanging by a thread. Determine never to surrender. Use love, patience, and forgiveness. Lay down your life and save your marriage. Maybe your kids are making dangerous decisions. Get down on your knees and fight like a man — of God!

Learn how to fight with faith, with prayer, and with the Word of God. Then, when your enemy attacks, fight for the righteous cause God gave you. Draw a line in the sand. Make your enemy pay. Make sure he gets the message. *Don't cross a warrior. Don't mess with this man of God.* Come out fighting.

And don't show up for this fight unarmed.

Use the weapons God gave you, and you'll win. Can you feel it? It's inside you.

It's time to fight like a man.

STRONG MEN
WITH WEAK WILLS

> We are not weak if we make a proper use of those
> means which the God of Nature has placed in
> our power.... The battle, sir, is not to the strong
> alone; it is to the vigilant, the active, the brave.
> —*Patrick Henry*

2.1

STRONG MEN WITH WEAK WILLS

Not long ago, three teenage boys flipped me off as they drove by and raced ahead, laughing hysterically at how much faster and cooler than me they were. Their smirks said it all: *Poor old geek dad driving his kids around in a soccer mom's SUV. No chance he'll ever catch us or do anything to us.*

Even though I had three of my six kids in the car, in that moment something snapped inside me. Almost without my realizing it, my foot pressed down on the accelerator and I was in hot pursuit. And I'd love to tell you that I'd hoped to wave them over and share God's love with them, but the truth is I was sizing them up. With a little training in various martial arts and at least twenty years of life experience on them, I was already planning how I could take them—all three of them. Without getting hurt or letting my kids get hurt, of course.

It must have been after a full two minutes of full-throttle car-chase mayhem (not unlike a car chase you'd see in a guy movie) that I came to my senses and let them go. Maybe it was because I caught the look of terror in my daughter's eyes in my rearview mirror. Maybe it was because I didn't want to have to explain to my wife why the kids and I were being held down at police headquarters. Maybe it was because I realized that I live in a rather small town and have a high profile as a pastor, one who usually doesn't engage in high speed chases (with his kids along) just to teach three punks a lesson.

Obviously, I'm not telling you this story to impress you with my self-control. Instead I hope you'll know that I'm as human as the next guy. One minute I can be seeking God in prayer. The next minute I'm in an unnecessary argument with my wife. I can worship passionately at church, only to gossip to a friend on the drive home. Occasionally, I've been known to preach a passionate, Spirit-filled message. But most days I wonder if I'll ever get it right.

Not only is it hard to serve God when things are going my way, it's even harder to be faithful to him when things *don't* go my way. You know what I'm talking about. You try to get ahead financially, but then your car or your air conditioner or your dishwasher breaks down, and you slip even farther behind. You work with all your heart to get promoted into your dream job, only to get passed over for that annoying guy you can barely stand. More and more it seems that when you decide to live for God with all your heart, all hell breaks loose in your life.

Which makes it really hard to do what you know you want to do — be a good husband, a great dad, a true friend, and, like David, a man after God's own heart. But when it feels like the deck is stacked against you, it's tough to follow through. It's hard to feel like you're really a godly man.

And let's be honest: if we look around, it often seems like there's a shortage of godly men. One of the most tragic verses in the Bible is probably Ezekiel 22:30, where God says, "I looked for someone among them who would build up the wall and stand before me in the gap on behalf of the land so I would not have to destroy it, but I found no one."

No one.

Not one.

God could not find one man who would stand for his people. If God were looking for a man like that today, I think he'd say something like this: "I'm looking for a man of integrity. I'm looking for a man with courage, a man willing to stand up for those who can't defend themselves. I'm looking for a man who will lay down his life for his wife, just like Christ laid down his life for his bride, the church. I'm looking for a man who will impart spiritual truth into the next generation. I'm looking for a man who will unselfishly care for others."

I hope that if God were looking for a man like this today, he wouldn't come up empty-handed. I hope he would find many men whose hearts beat only for him.

Are *you* a man like that?

Do you want to be?

2.2

SUPER POWERS

As I think about the men in the Bible whose lives seem to speak into my own, I'm always impressed by guys like Moses and Abraham, Joseph and David, Peter and Paul. They all provide me with examples and encouragement, insight and wisdom, persevering even when they screwed up. And there's the perfect example of the greatest man who ever walked this earth, Jesus, God's own Son.

But sometimes those guys — even Christ — can seem distant and removed from the problems you and I face — the constant demands on our time, the bills, the problems, the conflicts at work, the tensions at home, the struggles within our hearts. That's why I was surprised to find myself identifying so strongly with a guy whose story isn't known for having a happy, walking-with-God kind of ending. He's described as the strongest man who ever lived, and he's famous for being the male half of an infamous couple.

After studying his life, I'm convinced that most of us men are more like Samson than we might expect. And I'm not just talking about his pecs and his luxurious Troy Polamalu hair. Samson had so much potential, so many strengths beyond just his physical power, and yet his weaknesses continued to get the best of him.

Can you relate?

You've probably at least heard about Samson—even if only from a children's version of the story of Samson and Delilah—and his supernatural brawn, and how when his long hair was cut, he lost his strength. (I encourage you to read about Samson for yourself in Judges chapters 13–16.)

Although Samson's accomplishments are legendary, he's notorious for his weaknesses. Even with tremendous God-given potential, again and again he made bad decisions, ultimately sabotaging the life he could have had. God gave Samson unique abilities he could have used to advance God's kingdom. But because of his vanity—and selfishness and lust and shortsightedness—Samson squandered them. I can sum up Samson's life in just one statement: he was an incredibly strong man with a dangerously weak will.

What I hope you'll see is that God has given you, just like he gave Samson, special strengths that you can use to advance his kingdom, both in your life and in the lives of the people around you. I believe that we can learn enough from Samson's life to avoid making his mistakes.

Samson's story begins in Judges 13. Because the Israelites had been unfaithful to God, God let them fall under the rule of their enemies, the Philistines. But after the Israelites had served as Philistine subjects for forty years, God essentially said, "I think you've had enough, Israel. I'm raising up a man, Samson, who will deliver you from your bondage." This example reminds us that when God does something on earth, he usually does it through his people, and often through the men he calls to be his warriors.

So God sent an angel to a couple who hadn't been able to have any children. The angel told the woman that she was going to have a son, so she needed to start taking really good care of her health. Samson's parents couldn't know it yet, but from the beginning of their son's life, the Spirit of the Lord would stir within him, and God would give him supernatural strength. The angel didn't tell them that, but he *did* tell them something else pretty unusual. He told Samson's mother she should never let her son's hair be cut, because God wanted him to be a Nazirite, "dedicated to God from the womb."

As the Bible describes in Numbers 6, a Nazirite was an Israelite who wanted to devote himself or herself to God, but who was not born into the tribe of Levi (God's specially ordained priests). They could dedicate themselves to the Lord, taking a special vow and giving themselves to him. Such people would make the declaration, "I choose to live according to these vows and to serve God with my life."

There were three vows you had to make to become a Nazirite:

1. *Don't get drunk.* No Coronas. No martinis. No margaritas with your Mexican food. You couldn't even let alcohol touch your lips.
2. *Don't touch anything dead.* According to laws God had given the Hebrews, dead things were "unclean." God is perfect and holy, so Nazirites were forbidden to handle the remains of anything dead.
3. *Don't ever cut your hair.* You had to let your hair grow as long as it would grow naturally. You could style it; you just couldn't cut it. After doing some research, I'm convinced no Nazirite *ever* had a mullet, and especially not Samson. (Mullets are unholy hairstyles. But even if you had a mullet back in '82, there is room at the cross for you.)

Why long hair? Today when a person devotes their life to Christ, we celebrate by baptizing them. When you get baptized, that's a way that you can outwardly declare your testimony of an inward, spiritual transformation. You're telling people, "I'm aligning my life with Christ. This is who I am now." While baptism is a one-time event, a Nazirite's long hair was a constant reminder of his commitment to God. Just like my wedding ring is an outward, always-visible sign that I'm committed to my wife, a Nazirite's long hair was an outward, always-visible sign that he was set apart for God. If you saw a person with unusually long hair during Samson's time, you'd recognize, "Oh, that's a Nazirite! That guy's dedicated his life to God."

Of course, Samson wasn't just your run-of-the-mill Nazirite. Because of God's commitment to release his people from Philistine oppression, God placed his hand on Samson, filling his body with supernatural strength. How cool is that? Samson was sort of the first superhero. At least, he clearly had divinely given superpowers.

You might be thinking that Samson's life is about as far from yours as you can imagine. He doesn't drink. He's got all his hair (without Rogaine). And he's blessed with superstrength.

But think for a minute. You have strengths that God has given you to use in serving him and loving those around you. As I've already shared, I believe one of the gifts that God has given you is a warrior's heart, an idea we'll explore for the rest of the book. But what has God blessed you with that you can identify in your life right now? Before we start looking at how our weaknesses cause us to risk so many of the good things in our lives, it's important to remember what those good things are.

You have gifts to use for God's glory. You are chosen and set apart. You have battles to fight. And you have the right weapons to fight with.

You have a fight you must win.

And you have God, who already has given you the victory.

KINDS OF KRYPTONITE

Did you ever read *Superman* as a kid, or at least see one of the various versions at the movies? You may remember that Superman's only weakness was kryptonite, chunks of rock and debris that came from his home planet, Krypton. In the old comic books, kryptonite was green and instantly drained Superman of all his powers. But then some writers got creative and started coming up with different varieties of kryptonite. The red variety had random, wacky effects on the Man of Steel, sometimes causing him to mutate into animals or insects. The black kind changed his personality and caused psychological problems.

Although Samson wasn't from Krypton, he definitely had several issues that preyed on his weaknesses. As we'll see, despite having so much going for him, despite being chosen by God and blessed with supernatural strength, Samson couldn't escape his flaws. For all the blessings in his life, he often was his own worst enemy.

Sound familiar? Can you relate?

Unfortunately, I believe most of us are a lot like Samson—minus the superstrength and long hair, of course. Just as Samson had potential for greatness, he squandered that potential again and again through foolish decisions. He gave in to his emotions instead of following God's leading. He lunged after immediate gratification instead of obeying God. And he lost sight of his blind spots, which ultimately cost him his sight.

Most guys today are no different. I can't tell you how many guys I've met who are really aggressive at work, type-A leaders who go and take charge of situations and conquer their marketplaces. They're business studs, kicking tail and taking names. Striking deals. Moving ahead. Getting promoted. Then these same guys, when they get home, crash on the couch and turn passive. They refuse to lead their families or help their kids discover their purpose in life. They don't hesitate to take the field in one setting, then bench themselves in another.

I also talk to guys all the time who are disciplined at committing themselves to their finances, their careers, their hobbies, their fitness. They commit to what they *want* to commit to, but they won't commit to a woman.

Some men spend hours researching and studying everything that interests them. What's the best rod and reel? What's the best kind of TV to buy? And where can I get the best deal? They'll spend hours worshiping at the altar of selfishness, but they won't spend five minutes studying God's Word to build themselves spiritually.

A lot of guys honestly, deeply love both God and the special women in their lives. And yet these same men, men who possess so many godly attributes, find themselves locked in a prison of lust. But they're paralyzed, too afraid or ashamed to ask for help. So they do what men have done for centuries. They fake it. They live one life publicly and another one privately. They smile godly and loving smiles, while inwardly they're consumed by a raging fire of lust.

All of these different guys have so much untapped potential, yet they're slowly self-destructing through a cascade of bad decisions. What destroys, devastates, and demeans so many potentially great men? Samson's life shows us the same three problems that have made strong men weak since the beginning of time:

Lust.
Entitlement.
Pride.

2.4

WANDER LUST

In my more than twenty-two years of ministry, every man I've
talked to, every warrior, has said that lust is, at the very least,
a real and potential danger. What makes fighting lust so chal-
lenging is that we're surrounded by a culture committed to fulfilling our lusts the same way we crave a hamburger and drive
through McDonald's. We're bombarded with the message, "You
can do whatever you want, look at whatever you want—as long
as it doesn't hurt anybody. There's nothing wrong with just a
little glimpse. You're just window-shopping. It doesn't hurt if
you don't touch."

The Bible disagrees. We read in Ephesians, "But among you
there must not be even a hint of sexual immorality, or of any kind
of impurity, or of greed, because these are improper for God's
holy people" (5:3).

Many men tend to justify having a secret life, a life that they
lead when they're alone. They think, *It's no big deal. I'm not hurting anyone. I haven't done anything wrong. Besides, this is how I cope
with things.* But in Matthew 5:27–28, Jesus raised the standard
even higher than just our actions. He made the stunning declaration that if you even *look* lustfully at another person, you've committed adultery—in your heart. What matters to God is not just
what we look at or what we touch but what our hearts focus on.

Samson, the he-man with a she-weakness, knew what we know all too well. We see it, we want it, we take it—at least in our minds. When you see something you desire, you know what happens in your mind. You feel that pull, and your heart says, *I want it. I need it. I have to get that. And I have to get it now.*

When even a very reasonable man finds himself motivated by lust, all his logic goes out the window. He lets his hormones hijack his reason, commitment, and willpower. I've talked to countless men who, in honest moments, confess different versions of the same story. *I saw a hot woman, and I didn't want to stare, but I felt compelled to look. I had to. I tried to turn away, but my eyes seemed to drift uncontrollably back to her, as if they had a mind of their own. I fought it, but I couldn't stop my mind from racing down that old familiar path. I imagined her naked. I had thoughts about sex. And it all happened in a matter of seconds.*

Sadly, most men can relate to at least parts of the visual and sexual struggles. But not all lust is sexual. Maybe what you crave is a promotion, a raise, or winning at work. The promotion, the money, and the victory consume your thoughts and overwhelm your soul. Maybe it's a new house, a new car, a new boat. You think about it in the morning, at lunch, and when you go to bed. Whatever it is for you, it takes everything you have to hold yourself back from plowing headlong after that thing.

Samson had the same problem. Judges 14:1–2 says, "Samson went down to Timnah and saw there a [smoking hot] young Philistine woman. When he returned, he said to his father and mother, 'I have seen a Philistine woman in Timnah; now get her for me as my wife.'"

I may have tweaked that just a little, but it's true. (In the Bible, Samson is a sucker for smoking-hot women again and again.) There's a lot happening in these two verses. Samson lived in

Zorah with his parents. Timnah was four miles away, in enemy Philistine territory. You might wonder what he was even doing there. He abandoned his friends to visit his enemies, where he found a forbidden woman. (God had told his people they couldn't intermarry with people who didn't worship him.)

Samson was just *looking* for trouble. Like a guy lustfully clicking on questionable internet sites or channel-surfing so he might "accidentally" stumble on something to feed his sexual hunger, Samson didn't care about consequences. Just as soon as he saw this girl, he forgot everything else.

I don't care what God says.

I don't care what Mom and Dad say.

I don't care what's right or wrong. I'm a man.

I've got desires.

I've got needs.

I want it.

Lust makes strong men weak. It's like a spark that becomes an inferno in seconds. It's like kryptonite dust that weakens the strongest superman. It's like acid poured on aluminum foil. It starts small like a virus and takes control.

Think about it. Guys don't *plan* to screw up everything that matters most. *I'm going to ruin my life this year. I think I'll start with a little pornography. I'll lust a little. That'll eventually lead to an affair. I'll get a messy divorce, my kids will lose respect for me, and I'll struggle the rest of my life.* No one thinks, *I'm going to get a sexually transmitted disease. Maybe I could get one of the big ones. I could die before I'm forty. Fantastic!*

Men don't plan to destroy themselves. The problem is that we have an enemy who does. His mission statement is to "steal, kill, and destroy" everything that matters to God. Warriors, if you don't have a battle plan, you're going to fall victim to your enemy's

Fight

battle plan. Watch for temptation. It's waiting for you. There are plenty of innocent-sounding websites that offer more than information. Many of them count on the fact that they sound similar to legitimate, nonerotic sites. There are plenty of women who are looking for a man like you—someone who's lonely, maybe a little insecure, looking for a woman to offer him some comfort. There are plenty of sexual catalysts that have become mainstream cultural icons: *Playboy*. Victoria's Secret. The *Sports Illustrated* swimsuit edition. *Fifty Shades of Grey*. You don't have to go looking for trouble like Samson did. It will come looking for you.

Years ago I was traveling to speak at a conference. While waiting for my connecting flight, I headed to the men's restroom to take care of business. When I walked into a stall, I saw a magazine on the floor. Not just any magazine. It wasn't a copy of *Newsweek* or *Christianity Today*. It wasn't yesterday's newspaper or a travel brochure. It was a glossy *Playboy* magazine, right there, face up, looking at me, free for the taking.

All at once I was flooded with an overwhelming rush of sexual temptation. I felt like a teenage boy again, one who'd just stumbled onto a gold mine. I wish I could tell you that I thought, *How sad. I'd better throw that away so some eight-year-old kid doesn't see something he shouldn't see.* Instead, I thought, *Wow! I'm all alone in a bathroom in an airport in another state with a* Playboy *magazine!* No one would ever know. No big deal. It was just there, waiting for me.

Although it was probably only a couple of seconds, it felt like I agonized for hours. But then somehow I quickly came back to the truth. My thinking sobered as I considered my wife, my church, and my calling. I grabbed the magazine, threw it into the trash, and ran out of the bathroom, back to meet the guy traveling with me.

You might wonder, What's the big deal? To me, opening that one door could be the beginning of the death spiral so many men succumb to. "For the lips of the adulterous woman drip honey, and her speech is smoother than oil; but in the end she is bitter as gall, sharp as a double-edged sword. Her feet go down to death; her steps lead straight to the grave" (Prov. 5:3–5). To be honest, I was tempted. But by the grace of God, I avoided the temptation. To this day, I'm convinced that was a trap set specifically for me.

Maybe you don't really struggle with lust that much. Maybe you think you're doing really well, and you think you have this one under control. First Corinthians 10:12 says, "So, if you think you are standing firm, be careful that you don't fall!"

Watch for temptation, even if you don't *feel* vulnerable.

What does a battle plan against lust look like? Deliberately build safeguards into your life. For example, our entire organization's internet usage is filtered and monitored. We don't get certain magazines at our house — women's magazines with sex articles and surveys, men's magazines with scantily clad people and thinly veiled "lifestyle" advice, or lingerie magazines (just in case I need to search for months for the perfect teddy for my wife for Valentine's Day). I don't counsel women. If I do meet with a female staff member, at least one door is open (often two), and another person is present, just to be safe. I don't travel alone, and never with another woman except my wife, for work or for any other reason. Be intentional. Protect your integrity.

We have to fight all our lustful desires, and fight to win. (So much so that we'll address this subject in even more detail in section 4.) We must remain vigilant with our hearts if we want to control our bodies.

I read once about how an Eskimo killed a wolf that had been terrorizing his livestock. He dipped a sharp knife in animal blood and froze it. Then he did it again, adding layer after layer of frozen blood to the knife. Then he placed this "blood popsicle" in the ground firmly by the handle, with the blade sticking up.

When the wolf came, it smelled the blood and started licking it. It licked and licked, and the frozen blood numbed its tongue. Eventually, it was licking the blade. But the warm blood from the wolf's tongue mixed with the blood on the knife, so he couldn't tell. He just kept licking, until his tongue was in ribbons. By the time he realized what he'd done, it was too late. He laid down and bled to death, right next to the trap.

That's exactly what lust can do in a life. "Do not lust in your heart after her beauty or let her captivate you with her eyes.... Can a man scoop fire into his lap without his clothes being burned? Can a man walk on hot coals without his feet being scorched?" (Prov. 6:25, 27–28).

What seems pleasant, pleasurable, and easy is actually a trap intended to take you out.

2.5

CROSSING THE LION

About ten o'clock one night, my dog was freaking out outside, and my kids came and got me. "Daddy! We think Sadie has caught something outside!" *Hmm, maybe a cat?* I thought and smiled to myself.

You may not know this about me, but cats don't like me (probably because I rarely have anything nice to say about them). Have you ever had a cat walk by you? What does it do? It selfishly rubs its pathetic cat body up against your leg, then lifts its tail as it walks by, giving you a clear view of its cat butt. Disgusting on every level. And besides, Scripture says that Satan roams around like a lion, linking Satan directly to the cat family. So the thought of our dog treeing a cat brought a little spark of joy to my otherwise quiet evening.

"Take heart, children," I reassured them. "And stay away from the windows. Dad's got this."

Arming myself with my nunchucks and iPhone flashlight app, I headed out on a search-and-destroy mission. I assessed the situation, and sure enough, Sadie had treed not our neighbor's housecat but a *bobcat*. As in almost a mountain lion, as in a freakish creature of snarling stealth and insidious intelligence. As in another good reason for me to hate all cats.

Since I couldn't reach the beast with my nunchucks and I didn't feel like cutting down a tree right then, I decided just to take a picture instead. I steadied my iPhone and snapped a shot of it and its beady little eyes glaring evilly in the dark. Then *thud!* In the blink of an eye, stuff got real up in my back yard. The feline monster leaped from its perch to the ground, just a few feet from me.

Of course, I wasn't scared; I was "startled." While I'm eighty-seven percent sure I didn't say a curse word, I'm one hundred percent sure I *thought* one.

Fortunately, my ninja training kicked in, and before I even realized what was happening, I was back inside my house, with the doors locked and the blinds closed and all the lights on and my kids huddled around me, and we were all screaming and Amy was all, "What in the world is going on?" and we were all, "Mommyyy!"

Then I remembered that Sadie was still out there. Thankfully she survived and lived to hunt wild cats another day.

My lion story might be a little different from Samson's, but at least I have one.

Besides, all Samson did is what I'll do next time if I ever get another chance — he ripped his lion apart with his bare hands.

The story continues, "Samson went down to Timnah together with his father and mother. As they approached the vineyards of Timnah, suddenly a young lion came roaring toward him. The Spirit of the LORD came powerfully upon him so that he tore the lion apart with his bare hands as he might have torn a young goat.... Some time later, when [Samson] went back to marry [the Philistine woman], *he turned aside* to look at the lion's carcass, and in it he saw a swarm of bees and some honey. He scooped out the honey with his hands and ate as he went along" (Judg. 14:5–6, 8–9, emphasis mine).

Once again, this passage is just rich with lessons for us. First of all, the only reason Samson was in the position to make more mistakes was because he kept going back where he shouldn't have been (chasing Philistine skirts). But the main phrase I want you to focus on is "he turned aside."

Too many times, we're focused on some task, and then we turn aside. Even if we're doing what we're supposed to—probably *especially* if we're doing what we're supposed to—when we turn aside, it rarely ends well.

When Samson went to check out the lion he had killed, he found that bees had discovered the carcass and filled it with honey.

So he ate the honey.

That's disgusting.

Men are nasty. You know how a guy decides whether underwear on the floor is clean or dirty? You already know the answer to this question, don't you? He picks it up and sniffs it. Some guys, even if the underwear is dirty, will just turn it inside out and wear it again. Men. Are. *Nasty.*

But here's the most important thing we need to take away from this part of Samson's story: what was one of *the only three things* he had vowed not to do as a Nazirite?

"Don't touch anything dead."

That's not even a hard rule to follow. But Samson didn't just lightly touch something dead; he plunged his hands inside it *and then ate from it.*

Nasty.

With this senseless, selfish act, Samson betrayed the very God who had given him the power to rip the lion apart in the first place. And for what?

For a couple of fistfuls of honey.

What kind of an idiot is dumb enough to do that?

Me.

You.

You know it's true.

Men do dumber things every day.

We betray our God, who blessed us, for stupid, sinful things that we want in the moment, things that ultimately hurt us and the people we love.

Lust makes us think, *I want it*.

Entitlement is that little voice that takes "I want it" and adds "and I *deserve* it."

I work hard. I've earned some extra.

I've spent a lot of money at this place over the years. I deserve some payback.

Nobody else is taking care of my needs, so I've gotta do what I've gotta do.

Entitlement provides fuel for the engine of self-justification. But if we keep telling ourselves that we deserve to give in to temptation, eventually we're going to crash. And that crash could crush both you and those around you in ways you don't even want to dare to imagine.

2.6

---★---

PRIDE, NO PREJUDICE

---★---

Let's review Samson's vows again:

1. Don't get drunk.
2. Don't touch anything dead.
3. Don't ever cut your hair.

Not exactly rocket science there. But what does Mr. Strong do? "Now [Samson's] father went down to see the woman. And there Samson held a feast, as was customary for young men" (Judg. 14:10).

Why a feast? Even against the advice of everyone who knew him and loved him best, Samson did what men often do—exactly what *he* wanted to do. God's chosen man decided to marry the girl God had forbidden him to marry. When you put it like that, it seems pretty stupid, doesn't it? I mean, who wants to go and do the opposite of what God tells them? And yet we're no different from Samson, charging ahead and doing whatever we please.

The big guy was clearly dead-set on charging ahead. So on one hand, the feast made perfect sense. They're planning Samson's wedding, after all. But the word *feast* in this verse is the Hebrew word *mishteh* (mish-TEH). This wasn't a tea party with crumpets. The word means "feast," "drink," "banquet." It means

53

party. A *mishteh* is, by definition, a drinking occasion. Samson threw himself a kegger. He called in his buddies and they all got hammered.

His attitude says what many men say: "I'm a strong guy. I can handle a few drinks." The problem in this case, of course, is that he's not even supposed to drink *at all.* According to Numbers 6, Nazirites took their vows so seriously that not only did they not drink wine and fermented drinks but they didn't even "drink grape juice or eat grapes or raisins."

And then we have Mr. I Can Handle It here doing keg-stands.

I want it.

I deserve it.

I can handle it.

Before we judge Samson, let's be honest about ourselves. How many times have you seen a strong guy turn weak just like this? He thinks, *One hit's not going to kill me.* Or, *I'm just going to take one of these pills to see what it feels like.* Or, *I'll just stay for one drink.* He thinks, *I can handle it.* But before he even realizes it, some substance is handling him.

Maybe you've even been that guy.

Maybe substances aren't your thing. Maybe you're the guy who thinks, *Nice car! I could afford that.* Or, *Did somebody say "ski boat"?* Or, *This house just isn't big enough for our family anymore.* You think, *Sure, it'll be tight for awhile financially. But it'll be worth it. And besides, I deserve it. I can make payments. I can handle it.* Only, after awhile, that new ride doesn't have that "new car smell" anymore. Debt creeps in a little each month, and instead of enjoying your possessions, you start to feel more like they own you. You're not the master; you work for *them.*

I know a lot of guys who don't care about having more things. But when a pretty girl strolls by in a strappy little dress ... *Oooh,*

I know I'm not supposed to look, but I want *to!* Or the Christian guy says to his girlfriend, "Stay. Just a little longer. Let's just hold each other in our underwear and ... talk." Or he thinks, *I'll just look this one time. I can clear my internet history. Who's ever going to know? This will be the last time. I mean it.* These guys get caught in the snare of "I want it! Besides, I'm a good guy. I deserve a little sex break, a little treat, a little fun. It's just one time. I'm not hurting anybody. I can handle it." And before you know it, "handling it" is *exactly* what you're doing.

In another chapter, we'll get into detail about where Samson ends up. (Spoiler alert: it's not a good place.) Because of God's hand on him, with God's Spirit strengthening him from the moment he was born, Samson was perhaps the strongest man who ever lived. But because he squanders God's favor through his attitudes—lust, entitlement, pride—he ends up at rock bottom. His enemies gouge out his eyes and parade him around like some kind of sideshow freak for their sick entertainment.

The man who once killed thousands using nothing but the jawbone of a donkey and brute strength, laid low, humiliated, his prized hair long gone. He could have changed the world. He was chosen. He could have been a weapon for the kingdom of God. He *should* have been. Instead, his story is a footnote in history, a cautionary tale. But Samson himself chose where he ended up by betraying the One who loved him.

And you have the same choice to make.

If you fall prey to our enemy's schemes, like Samson did, am I saying you're going to end up just like him? I sure hope not. But you could do worse. Seriously. Just think about what *could* happen.

If you lose the fight against temptation, denying God's call on your life, ignoring the gifts he's given you, living for yourself instead of for the people he made you to stand in the gap for, you could be even worse off. It's really not even hard to picture it: You're in your forties or your fifties or your sixties. You look back on a failed marriage (or more than one) and realize, too late, *Idiot! So much of that was my fault. Why didn't I do something when I could? Why didn't I engage? Why didn't I fight? Why didn't I tell the truth? Ask for help? Confess my sins? I have to live the rest of my life with these regrets.*

I know plenty of guys whose kids are all grown now, but they won't come around at Christmastime. Is that where you're headed? That not only do your kids have no respect for you, they don't even want to be in your presence? What are you going to do *now* to keep that from happening *then?* Do you have the guts? Do you have what it takes to be God's man?

Maybe you're terrified. You've been living with secrets, and you don't see a way out. But let me share a huge truth from God's Word. In Luke 12:2–3, Jesus said, "There is *nothing* concealed that will not be disclosed, or hidden that will not be made known. What you have said in the dark will be heard in the daylight, and what you have whispered in the ear in the inner rooms will be proclaimed from the roofs" (emphasis mine).

That's real, man.

That's going to happen.

Would you rather be in control of that conversation, or have it happen *to* you?

It's so much better to confess your sins and enjoy forgiveness than to be caught in them. There may be a time in your future when your private life becomes public, and you dread seeing anyone because you're so humiliated by your actions. Let's not sugarcoat it, guys: that's where sin leads.

And you know it.

Of course, it doesn't have to go down that way.

If you choose to follow Christ, there is spiritual greatness within you, a strength to keep going and not stay down. God's power in your life is that no matter what you've done, you can be transformed. You can be new. You can make a difference in this world. You can be a godly man. You can be a godly husband. You can be a godly dad. No matter what's happened in the past, you can be God's man. But you do have to keep fighting. You can't give up.

You have to stop trying to do it in your own strength. Because our spiritual enemy, Satan, is an expert at making strong men weak.

Fortunately, and don't miss this, our good God specializes in making weak men strong.

And God is with you. And he is *for* you.   we it

The God we serve absolutely loves to make weak men strong. Paul tells us in 2 Corinthians 12:9–10, "[The Lord] said to me, 'My grace is sufficient for you, for my power is made perfect in weakness.' Therefore I will boast all the more gladly about my weaknesses, so that Christ's power may rest on me. That is why, for Christ's sake, I delight in weaknesses, in insults, in hardships, in persecutions, in difficulties. For when I am weak, then I am strong."

We've already talked about the attitudes that make strong men weak. Lust says, "I want it." Entitlement says, "I deserve it." And pride says, "I can handle it." But we can turn these around. Once we get our hands on our enemy's battle plans, we can turn them back on him and take our victory (2 Cor. 2:11).

Your enemy wants to take you out, through selfishness and shame, tricking you into trading your God-given power for things that tempt your fleshly appetites. But if we can just man up, if we can admit that we're weak and vulnerable, that we need

God's strength and his presence, then he'll redeem us and fill us with purpose and meaning.

You can be a man of spiritual strength, a man of integrity, a man of courage. You can be a man who defends the defenseless. You can be a man who serves his wife and his family. You can be a man who unselfishly gives to others.

You can be that man.

A warrior.

WEAK IS THE NEW STRONG

One time I was trying to shovel about twelve inches of packed snow off my driveway so I could get my car out and drive to church to preach. Knowing it was a big task, I started several hours early.

With all my strength, again and again, I struck the snow with my shovel. Cracking through the icy snow took considerably more effort than I imagined. Within half an hour, my hands started to blister, my back started to ache, and my face started to turn red, partly from the cold air, but more from frustration. An hour later, I had cleared only about one-tenth of what I'd need to even get my car out of the garage.

That's when my neighbor powered by, smiling joyfully on his tractor, moving snow like he was a child playing in a sandbox. "Need help?" he graciously (and miraculously) offered. (Angels in heaven sang. Not the naked ones playing harps. I'm talking the massive, Michael-the-kick-your-tail-archangel-singing-in-baritone type of angels.) In less than fifteen minutes, my driveway and half my street was cleared—not a flake of snow on the concrete.

I was struck by the contrast. My shovel and limited strength. Or a tractor and a skilled driver's strength. Fighting life's battles works the same way. You can fight using your own limited power. Or you can tap into the all-powerful, limitless God who wants to help you win every battle for his causes. Here's how:

1. *Turn "I want it" into "I want God."* Whatever "it" is for you, as soon as you start to feel that tug, that gravity drawing you toward "I want it," catch yourself. Resist the pull. Capture those thoughts and force them to be obedient to Christ (2 Cor. 10:3–5). What you really want is God—his strength, his daily power, his Word living inside you. You want him ordering your steps. You want his Spirit convicting you when you sin, correcting you, leading you in the paths of righteousness (John 16:7–8; Heb. 12:6; Ps. 23:3). Some people say God is a crutch for the weak. Absolutely! I'm weak. I want God. I need his strength. And so do you.

2. *Turn "I deserve it" into "I deserve death."* Extreme? Maybe. But you know what? This is war. And when the stakes are eternal life—yours and the lives of others—we're going to do whatever we have to do. We're unholy men who have sinned against a holy God. The payment for our sin is death (Rom. 6:21–23). We deserve death. This is God's universe; we just live in it. He doesn't owe us anything. We owe him everything. What did you make? Nothing. He made everything. For everything you have, you owe him. When we were still sinners, God sent his Son to save and forgive us (Rom. 5:6–8). When we can be humble enough to admit the truth, it should make us bow down before a holy God, saying, "I don't *have* to serve you. I *want* to serve you."

3. *Turn "I can handle it" into "I can't handle anything without God."* If you aren't a Christian, now is your moment to call on God. How are you doing without him? Ask Christ to forgive you and be your Savior, your Lord. You can't handle anything without him. If you are a Christian, do you remember what your life was like before you came to Christ? I remember mine. And let me tell you, I simply was not capable of righteousness. The best I could have come up with on my own was shameful before God (Isa. 64:6; Phil. 3:7–9). I *need* God. Every time you feel that pride creeping back in, that "I can handle this," remember what we deserve: death. We can't handle anything without God.

Again, I ask you, what kind of strength do you want to fight with? Your feeble strength? Or God's unlimited, unmatched power?

You are weak.

God is strong.

His strength is made perfect in your weakness.

Satan loves to make strong men weak.

God loves to make weak men strong.

Will you let him?

SPIRIT-LED
NOT EMO-DRIVEN

Feelings are much like waves. We can't stop them
from coming, but we can choose which one to surf.
—*Jonatan Mårtensson*

SPIRIT-LED, NOT EMO-DRIVEN

We men don't like to think of ourselves as being emotional. Women are emotional, not us. We're strong; we're logical; we're thinkers. The truth is, all humans are emotional beings. And that's a good thing. God made us with the capacity for emotions, so having emotions is not a liability. It's not a sin to *feel*. We can't prevent ourselves from feeling what we feel. Where we get into trouble is when we allow those emotions to drive our actions.

For example, I'm a grown-up, but you wouldn't know it from my behavior sometimes. A few years ago, we had our church offices at a little strip mall. One day, outside my office window I noticed a large group of high school kids starting to gather. All of a sudden, two boys just started beating on each other. The intensity of their rage shimmered like heat waves off the pavement.

So what did *I* do? I called out to the other pastors, "Fight! Fight!" and I ran outside to watch. With God as my witness, for probably a full thirty seconds, I stood there acting like I was at a UFC event. One guy clearly had the advantage in size and weight; I decided he was the Instigator. But the other guy—the Underdog, in my mind—was quick and agile, dodging the Instigator's wild swings and getting in a few sharp jabs. Overall, they were well matched.

Then I remembered, "Craig, you're a grown-up. You're a pastor. You don't encourage fights; you break them up." *Oh, yeah.* So I ran up to the fighters and grabbed one. I was pulling him off when it occurred to me, *If all these kids turn on me, this could go really badly.* Fortunately, one kid yelled, "It's Pastor Craig! Run!" And they did.

What is it about watching someone else's fight that is so mesmerizing? My heart was pumping and adrenaline was coursing through my veins, and I might as well have been chasing punks with our Suburban or standing up to Bo Talbot on the playground. I was into it. I was excited! But then, thankfully, the voice of reason—also frequently known as the Holy Spirit—reminded me of something more important than how I felt: who I am.

Not just a warrior but God's warrior.

3.2

SHOOT FIRST

Even though both men and women have emotions, we process them differently. Generally speaking, women talk, while men act. Most of the time, when a woman is upset about something, she'll talk about it. And talk and talk and talk. Most men don't do that. (One article I read said men on average speak about seven thousand words a day, while women say twenty thousand words a day—with gusts up to thirty thousand!) When we get frustrated, something's about to go down. Men act.

Sometimes when Amy needs to process some difficult emotions, she'll invite one of her female friends over to talk (usually for hours). I have never in my life had a dude call me and say, "Hey Craig, could you come over to my house and sit with me for half a day on my sofa and drink some tea so we can talk?" If a guy did that, we wouldn't be friends anymore.

For most men, talking doesn't feel like it accomplishes anything. "Doing" does. The problem is that when we let our emotions lead us to do something, often it is something we shouldn't have done.

The problem most of us face is that we just act on our emotions. While being emotion-driven often leads us to do the ungodly thing, being Spirit-led *never* does. If you truly want to do what's right, letting your emotions take over will rarely get you the outcome you want.

I don't know how this plays out at your house. Maybe you want to engage more with your kids. But you work hard all day, and then once you get home, you're just mentally drained and emotionally fried. The path of least resistance is always calling. You find yourself sitting down for just a minute to turn on the TV. Thirty minutes stretches into an hour that drifts into four, and before you know it, it's bedtime. Worst of all? That's not even what you wanted to do.

Maybe you slip up and say something stupid, something you didn't even mean to say. You know you should apologize, but you figure, "Man, if I open that door, there's no telling what all might come spilling out." Or you're caught up in your spirit of entitlement—"*I* shouldn't be the one to apologize; *she's* the one who got mad"—so you let your pride keep you from doing what you know in your heart is right. That's being emotion-driven, not Spirit-led.

Maybe it's not you who does something stupid but somebody close to you. When you can just be yourself, you're an easygoing guy. Nobody *wants* to explode in anger. But in that moment, it feels like you can't even help it. That volcano erupts out of you, and you're just kind of a bystander watching it happen.

It's like your default setting kicks in—the fight or flight impulse—and to feel like a "real man" (according to cultural standards, not necessarily God's), most guys choose to fight.

Yes, I'm convinced God made us men to be warriors—all the more reason we must be led by his Spirit. We need to know what, when, where, and how to fight. We need to fight for what's right. That's why we can't trust our emotions to guide us. It's like deciding to shoot first while blindfolded. You're reacting while you can't even see your target to aim properly.

Paul describes this tendency in Romans 7:15 and 19: "I do not understand what I do. For what I want to do I do not do, but what I hate I do.... For I do not do the good I want to do, but the evil I do not want to do — this I keep on doing."

Why do we give in to the instincts that create the results we despise? Because we let ourselves be emotion-driven, not Spirit-led. Fortunately, in Galatians 5:16 – 17, Paul offers a solution to the struggle: "Live by the Spirit, and you will not gratify the desires of the sinful nature. For the sinful nature desires what is contrary to the Spirit, and the Spirit what is contrary to the sinful nature. They are in conflict with each other, so that you do not do what you want" (NIV 1984).

Being led by the Spirit is a choice we make. We allow God's Spirit to lead, and then we go where he directs us.

Simple, right?

Well, we probably all know that's what we *should* do.

But in reality, so many men end up doing what they *shouldn't* when they let their emotions drive them.

RIDDLE ME THIS

Samson is the original emo-driven poster boy. As we jump back to his story, watch what happens when he lets his feelings drive his actions instead of following God's guidance. Remember, Samson had decided he was going to marry a Philistine woman. While there was a lot wrong with this scenario, probably the biggest issue was that she worshiped false gods. But as we've already seen, that didn't stop Samson. He didn't care what God or his parents said. He saw her, he wanted her, and he was going to have her.

When we last left Samson, he had just snacked on a little honey out of a lion carcass, and he was about to wash that down with some adult beverages at his bachelor party. There were thirty other guys there with him, all Philistines, enemies of Israel who actually hated him. (But everybody's your buddy at a party, right?) Samson decides he wants to have a little fun with them, so he says, "Let me tell you a riddle."

Unfortunately, Samson's a typical dude, which means that he can't just have fun without turning it into a competition. And what's the best way to make any competition more interesting? You guessed it—a bet. Samson adds, "If you can give me the answer within the seven days of the feast, I will give you thirty linen garments and thirty sets of clothes. If you can't tell me the answer, you must give me thirty linen garments and thirty sets of clothes" (Judg. 14:12 – 13).

Like so many other guys you probably know, just because Samson could bench-press an ox cart didn't mean he was good at math. He's dealing with thirty guys here. If he wins, each guy has to come up with only one outfit. But if he loses, he has to come up with *thirty* outfits. (Of course, Samson probably didn't think he could lose; no guy will ever play a game unless he believes he's going to win.)

Here's his riddle: "Out of the eater, something to eat; out of the strong, something sweet" (v. 14).

You and I know exactly what he's talking about because we have information that his Philistine party buds don't. We know that Samson destroyed a lion ("the eater" and "the strong") and that later he ate honey out of its body ("something to eat" and "something sweet"). Of course, the reason nobody else knows about it is because Samson didn't *want* anyone knowing about it; it meant revealing that he had violated two of his three Nazirite vows before God. Samson gave them his riddle, but, Scripture says, "For three days they could not give the answer."

Of course, they got really ticked when they couldn't figure it out. What they did next was predictable, although insanely vicious. They were countrymen of Samson's fiancée, and they felt like she was betraying them by letting this Israelite meathead make them look bad. So they went to her and said, "Coax your husband into explaining the riddle for us, or we will burn you and your father's household to death."

That sounds reasonable.

Samson's fiancée went straight for the thermonuclear option, every woman's greatest weapon: she cried. When in doubt, cry. (It works on me every time—and on most traffic cops.)

"You don't really love me!" she sobbed.

She kept this up for seven days, until Samson finally caved. He told her his secret, which led to verse 18: "Before sunset on the seventh day the men of the town said to him, 'What is sweeter than honey? What is stronger than a lion?'"

Samson was furious. He had no doubt in his mind how they figured it out. After all, his fiancée was the only other person alive who knew: "Samson said to them, 'If you had not plowed with my heifer, you would not have solved my riddle.'"

I wondered if this might have been some kind of popular phrase during Samson's time, a phrase with a deeper meaning, maybe like, "You can't judge a book by its cover." I looked it up in Hebrew, and here's what it *actually* says: "If you had not plowed with my heifer, you would not have solved my riddle."

I find two principles I think we can all take away from this phrase, two lessons I'd like you to internalize:

1. Never let anyone "plow" with your wife.
2. Never call your wife a heifer.

I've been married for almost two and a half decades now, so you can trust me; both of these are rock-solid bits of advice.

3.4

ANGER MANAGEMENT

Samson blows past opportunity after opportunity to respond to his circumstances through the prompting of the Holy Spirit. The mistake he keeps making is to let himself be emotion-driven, rather than Spirit-led. In verse 19 we read, "Then the Spirit of the LORD came powerfully upon him. He went down to Ashkelon, struck down thirty of their men, stripped them of everything and gave their clothes to those who had explained the riddle. *Burning with anger,* he returned to his father's home" (Judg. 14:19, emphasis mine).

So basically, immediately after he lost this bet, Samson strolled into a nearby town to do a little shopping. He picked an innocent guy who happened to be wearing clothes, murdered him, then took his clothes. Once he'd killed thirty men, he took all of their clothes back to the party and handed them out to pay off his gambling debt. Finally, he left his own engagement party, "burning with anger," and went home to Zorah.

The next thing that happened might seem pretty strange to us today: "Samson's wife was given to one of his companions who had attended him at the feast. Later on, at the time of wheat harvest, Samson took a young goat and went to visit his wife. He said, 'I'm going to my wife's room.' But her father would not let him go in. 'I was so sure you hated her,' he said, 'that I gave her to your companion'" (14:20 – 15:2).

You read that right. While Samson was gone from his engagement celebration on his murder minivacation (and who knows how long it takes to kill thirty men, get their clothes, and make it back?), the bride's father was embarrassed that his future son-in-law had just disappeared. It wouldn't have been uncommon at that time to say, "Well, she's of marrying age, and her fiancé is not here, so I'm going to give her to another man." And that's exactly what her father did.

The Scriptures don't tell us what Samson was thinking, but apparently at least some significant time had passed, because he didn't return until "the time of wheat harvest." And since we don't know when the engagement party started, we don't know how much later this was.

Even against the backdrop of what a hothead Samson has been, you really couldn't guess what he would do next. If you thought he was cranky when he left before, you haven't seen anything yet. Upon learning his father-in-law had given his fiancée to somebody else, he flew into a rage. He caught three hundred foxes, tied their tails together in pairs, put torches between their tails, lit them, and then turned them loose in the Philistine's crops. They lost everything: grain, vineyards, olive groves.

Because this was an agricultural society, this single act of destruction ravaged their economy. Now it was the Philistines' turn to be enraged. When they discovered that Samson was responsible, an angry mob stormed his fiancée's father's house, then burned him and his daughter to death. Just as we've seen happen to so many other men, here's yet another example of how Samson's emotion-driven fits cost him everything he cared about.

For a lot of men, anger is a default emotion. Think about it. When someone embarrasses us, rarely do we feel *only* embarrassment. Most of the time, that embarrassment also makes us angry. *Nobody's gonna make me look like a fool. They'll be sorry they ever messed with me.*   *Different*

If a woman stubs her toe on a chair, she might sit down on that same chair to rub her foot. But if a man stubs his toe on a chair, what does he do? He kicks the chair *again.* "I hate you, you stupid chair!" (And that's the clean version of what most men tell the chair.) That's because when men experience something negative, anger is usually our automatic response.

What did Samson have to be angry about anyway? Let's replay this sequence of events:

Samson is the one who pursues the wrong woman.

He's the one who decides to marry that woman.

He's the one who ignores his parents' advice and God's wisdom.

He's the one who taunts the Philistines with a riddle.

He's the only one who knows the secret.

He's the one who gives the secret away.

He's the one who leaves his wife at the altar to go kill a bunch of guys.

He's the one who sets fire to the crops.

Samson was mad at the world, but in reality, almost everything that happened *was his own fault.* At any point, Samson could have backed off, even just a little. If he had just taken a minute to cool off, maybe he even could have turned things around. Instead, over and over, he escalates every situation, forcing others to react.

What about you? Can you relate to Samson? Do you ever feel angry at the world? You're the victim. Life isn't fair. Why don't you get the breaks other guys seem to get?

How much of that do you think might be *you?*

Have you ever thought, *I hate my boss. This is such a pointless job?* In reality, maybe you felt frustrated because you didn't finish college, or you accepted a job that you felt was beneath you. Is it possible you're actually mad at yourself, and you're just taking it out on someone else?

Have you ever thought, *My wife won't meet my physical needs?* In reality, you haven't met any of her emotional needs in months. Maybe you should recognize that her distance is a natural consequence of your actions.

Have you ever thought, *I'm so mad at God. I shouldn't have to go through this. I didn't ask for this life?* In reality, you may be in the circumstances you're in right now because of your own unwise decisions, and you're just blaming it on God.

Listen, I've been there. I've thought each one of these things during different seasons in my life. And why? Because I was letting myself be driven by anger, rather than letting the Spirit lead me.

What are some of the ways your anger has driven you? Can you call it what it is? Can you admit you need help? That you need forgiveness? Maybe it's time you asked some of your friends to help you. "Would you pray for me? Would you hold me accountable? Would you go shoot hoops with me so I can feel good about beating someone?"

Picture each person who has been hurt by your anger. Are you man enough to apologize? To own your part? To take responsibility for your actions? Maybe it's time you gave some thought to what you should say to them.

Your spouse: "Honey, I've taken out my frustrations on you. I'm sorry."

Your children: "Kids, I haven't treated you as well as I should have. I haven't managed my anger. It wasn't your fault. It was mine."

Your friends: "I've come around only when I needed something. I haven't been there when you needed me. I haven't been a good friend to you."

Then follow up with the hardest part: "Can you please forgive me? I know I don't deserve your forgiveness. But I'd be honored to have it. Will you forgive me?"

You're going to be tempted to try to explain yourself, to justify your actions.

"Things have just been really tough lately."

"I've been under a lot of stress."

"If *you* would have just ..."

Don't do that. Fight the temptation to make excuses. Own your part. Own what *you* can do to make a change.

"I have not treated you with honor and respect. I want to be a faithful man of God. I want to be led by the Spirit, not driven by my emotions."

Anger was one of Samson's issues, as it is for most men. But anger has some equally destructive siblings: pride and despair.

SLINGING JAWBONES

After the Philistines killed Samson's fiancée and her father, Samson killed a bunch of their men and vowed to keep wreaking vengeance on them. So in Judges 15:9, a Philistine horde went looking for Samson, setting up camp near Lehi in the land of Judah. Samson's irresponsibility had finally put his own people, the tribe of Judah, in a really bad spot. Remember, whatever the Israelites thought of the Philistines, the Philistines were still their rulers. So Samson pretended to surrender himself to his people, allowing them to give him over to the Philistines. But really, he was just playing both sides. He took his strength — a gift from God — for granted, using it to continue to wage his furious campaign of revenge. He let the Israelites tie him up, and then when the Philistines came to get him, Samson broke the ropes that bound him, and "finding a fresh jawbone of a donkey, he grabbed it and struck down a thousand men" (15:15).

Think about how arrogant this was. It was like UFC on steroids times a thousand, channeling the power of God. I have no doubt that on a good day I could take out three high school boys by myself (the three small ones who were flipping me off, anyway). And if I had my nunchucks, I could easily take out half a dozen. But ten? Probably not. Fifteen? No way!

SPIRIT-LED, NOT EMO-DRIVEN 79

When Samson killed a thousand enemies, there was no doubt that it was the power of God that made it possible. All credit has to go to God. With God, nothing is impossible. If that's what God wants done, it will happen in his power. But in verse 16, Samson takes all the credit: "Samson said, 'With a donkey's jawbone *I* have made donkeys of them. With a donkey's jawbone *I* have killed a thousand men'" (emphasis mine).

Of course, there's another word for donkey, so the Bible translators are really just being nice. But Samson was mocking the people he had just defeated, and he called them that other word that means donkey. (In case you're wondering, it rhymes with like *grass*.)

If you're thinking you'd never respond like Samson did, think again. Consider all the things we do and say when we want to impress people:

"Hey guys, watch this!" (A lot of guys say this right
    after they ask someone to hold their beer, but that's a
    discussion for another time.)
"How you like me now?"
"Here's a picture of me with [LeBron James, Angelina
    Jolie, Billy Graham, President Obama, or — if they're
    really trying to impress you — all of the above]."
"Check out this picture of my girlfriend. She's a model.
    She lives in Canada."
"Hey, did you hear? I got the promotion! Yeah, I
    know — crazy to think about how much I'll be pay-
    ing in taxes next year. Whew!"

For me it's, "You won't believe how many people God brought to our church this weekend." (Translation: I'm really proud of the attendance at church because it makes me feel good about myself, so I'm going to tell you, but give God "credit" so I have permission to brag.)

Yep, we all have our own favorite jawbones that we sling around to try to build ourselves up. Basically we're saying, "Yes-sir, here's the evidence. Because I've done this, been there, bought this, know that person, and get to do what I do, I'm a superior kind of guy." Not so pretty when you think about it. Nobody likes a showoff, so we try to disguise it, sometimes with false humility. "No, really, I have to credit my team. I only get to lead the best team there is, and they're the ones who landed this account."

Why do so many of us battle pride? Pride is always born of our insecurities. When we don't know who we are in Christ, we use pride to try to fill that void. James 4:6 says, "God is opposed to the proud, but gives grace to the humble" (NASB). And Prov-erbs 16:18 warns, "Pride goes before destruction, a haughty spirit before a fall."

So many of us try to define ourselves by our accomplish-ments, to find our worth in what we've done, instead of in whom we belong to. We want to rely on our achievements, our vic-tories, our trophies, our wins to define us instead of acknowl-edging God as the source of all good things in our lives. Like Samson, we want to take the credit and be known as a winner, a beast, a leader, a man's man, "somebody."

Pride can be intoxicating. But the hangover is hell. We're human; we do have (many) limitations, and we must rely on God. When we lose sight of our identity and get spiritual amnesia, we often feel like we're drowning in our emotions. And it's not just the storms of anger and pride that can capsize us. On the surface, we can appear calm and in control, even as an emotional riptide pulls us under and into the depths of despair.

///////////////////////////////★///////////////////////////////

DROWNING IN DESPAIR

///////////////////////////////★///////////////////////////////

Maybe you don't struggle with controlling your anger or feel like you're particularly arrogant or conceited. Maybe you never talk about your accomplishments or throw jawbones or display your trophies. Maybe the emotion that seems to be in control of your actions is a chronic dull sadness, a sense of loneliness that's trying to swallow you up. You might not even realize what's going on, only that you're not yourself anymore. That you have no hope.

Many factors can contribute to despair. Maybe it's because you've simply worn yourself slap out. You work a full-time job supporting your family, then spend evenings and weekends working on the house and the yard. Or maybe you work several jobs trying to make ends meet through college, then do fraternity projects and play sports with your buddies. Maybe you're single, keeping up an active social life, and you never crash into bed before midnight. Maybe the reason why you're so depressed is you've been burning yourself out.

Sometimes it's not even all that we have done that wears us out but thinking about all we have to do in the future. A few Mondays ago, I walked lifelessly into my office, feeling hungover from preaching all weekend long. While I was exhausted from weeks of nose-to-the-grindstone work, it was everything around the corner that consumed my thoughts.

I had seven more weekends to do before having a weekend off, six ministry trips, our annual three-day all-staff event, too many meetings to count, and—oh, yeah—this book to complete. After just glancing at my to-do list, I felt paralyzed, frozen by fear. Certainly I couldn't do it all. No one could. I tried to fight back the tears. My emotions won. The tears flowed against my will.

I was exhausted.

That stress you're feeling isn't necessarily just from physical exertion. It's more like you feel the weight of your responsibilities—being there for family and friends, never wanting to let anybody down, living up to your parents' expectations, earning enough to pay all the bills. You try to be strong for everybody, to be the provider, the glue holding everyone's lives together. Maybe you even feel like your life makes all of their lives possible. If you're carrying that burden, no wonder you're exhausted. Acknowledging it is the first step in overcoming it.

Another common cause of despair is shutting out people who matter. Samson took pride in the fact that he was self-sufficient and needed no one's help. Whether he was showing off or seeking revenge, he was committed to being a one-man show. A lot of us men do the same thing when we start feeling overwhelmed. Our actions communicate, "I'm not letting you in. I won't share what's going on with me. Even if I tried, you wouldn't understand." We push people away, then put up a wall, then dig a moat, then set out emotional land mines that go off when people we care about step on them.

Honestly, I'm speaking from experience. Exhaustion sucks me into withdrawal almost every time. Getting tired kicks on my withdrawal autopilot. Almost as soon as I start feeling the dull pain of that burden, I start stacking up bricks, one on top of another. I used to believe that's just what men do. People get too close to our emotions, and that touchdown-run stiff-arm pops out: "I'm tough. I'll deal with this myself." Later in my life, I justified it with, "People who haven't been leaders probably couldn't even understand what I'm feeling." Eventually, I had to just get real and admit it was pride. Notice all the I's in those reactions? (But *you've* probably never felt like that, right?)

Tired and alone, the snare most men find themselves falling into is predictable: You start feeling like all the forces in the universe are aligning against you. You focus on negatives. You feel alone. You feel depressed. You feel defeated.

If there's one thing you can count on self-pity for, it's exaggeration. Every time you start thinking about how bad things are, it's like a game to make sure everything is as bad as it *could* be. You'll catch yourself using extreme words like *never, always,* and *forever:*

> *I've never been any good.*
> *I'm always going to be stuck in this life.*
> *Things are never going to get any better.*
> *I'm never going to get that promotion now.*
> *After this mistake, my wife is never going to forgive me.*
> *My kids will never follow Jesus when they see what a hypocrite*
>   *I've been.*

We get stuck in these negative loops of self-judgment and condemnation that are not from God. His Spirit always leads us to confession, to changing directions and going God's way, to a fresh start, to grace. Often God has forgiven us, but our emotions haven't caught up. I'm convinced this is just another form of our pride — wanting to be in control of ourselves and not rely on

God. We'd rather hate ourselves than risk the vulnerability and humility required to depend on him. It seems easier to expect the worst than to put our hope in God.

Despair often comes from our not wanting to reveal our weaknesses to others. We don't want to admit to ourselves that we need God. Why do men refuse to ask for directions? Because we don't have the courage to tell anyone we need help.

We'd rather drown in despair than grab hold of the lifeline that God always extends to us.

ALL ABOUT ME

Why is this such a problem for men? Why do we sometimes seem to prefer relying on our emotions rather than trusting God and following the leading of his Spirit? I believe it's because most of us want to be the hero, the main character, the center of the story that we're telling about ourselves.

We want everything to be about us.

And that's the problem. Because God is always the main character of the story. He's the center.

Everything is about him—even us.

Once we acknowledge that God is the main character, only then can we even begin to get to that place where we're no longer tempted to let our emotions drive us. We'll actually *want* to be led by the Spirit.

If you're continually driven by your emotions, you're going to end up just like Samson: a man with divine potential trapped in a cycle of self-destruction. But if you're willing to sacrifice your emotions on the altar, committing them to God, then you make him the main character in your story. You'll still feel your emotions, just like always, but they won't drive you anymore. You'll finally escape the slavery of impulse and enter into the freedom that comes only from being led by the Spirit of God.

I dare you to ask yourself, "What does God really want for me?" Do you think he wants you to be driven by your emotions, or to be freed to follow his Spirit? And what about you? Ask yourself, "What do I *really* want?" Do you honestly want to continue to be driven by your emotions? Wouldn't you rather be a man of integrity, a man of character, a man of deep spiritual strength? Just imagine if, in every decision you made, you had the confidence that you were doing just what God wanted you to do, the conviction that you were acting as his ambassador.

I know you've blown it. (We all have!) I know you've had thoughts — maybe even done things — that you'd be ashamed to tell anyone about. There's that dark secret you've been keeping, that thing that no one else knows about, and you worry all the time that if anybody found out, you'd never recover from the damage. You think, *My wife would never forgive me if she knew the truth.* Or, *If my kids knew, they'd never look at me the same way.* Or, *I'd never be able to rebuild trust if they found out about what I really did.*

Maybe.

Or maybe there's great news that you just haven't been in a position to consider: You're in need. If you will just acknowledge that need once and for all before a holy God who loves you, then this could be the greatest day of your life. If you let your need drive you to God, God will meet your deepest need.

That's exactly what happened to Samson. Even though he had turned his back on God. Even though he had betrayed two of his three Nazirite vows. Even though he had constantly let his anger and pride dictate his actions. When he cried out to God in genuine need, the God who loved him had mercy and compassion on him.

Samson had just killed a thousand men. At first, still caught up in the victory, he was proud of himself, as though he could have done it without the supernatural strength that came from God. But once the moment was over, when his blood cooled, he realized the position he had put himself into. Standing there, surrounded by all those bodies, covered in their blood, it dawned on him: *This could be the end of me. If the Philistines catch me here in this desert, they're going to kill me. Or I may even just die of thirst out here before that.*

In that moment, he allowed his need to drive him to God: "He cried out to the Lord, 'You have given your servant this great victory. Must I now die of thirst and fall into the hands of the uncircumcised?' Then God opened up the hollow place in Lehi, and water came out of it. When Samson drank, his strength returned and he revived" (Judg. 15:18–19).

The first thing that happened was that as soon as Samson realized his need, he came to his senses. He admitted that he wasn't the one who had defeated the Philistines; it was God. Once he humbled himself, he was able to describe his need to God in his own words. And when he did, Samson returned God to his rightful place in his story: at the center.

And then, "his strength returned and he revived."

When you return to God and give your weakness to him, only then will your strength return. But it's ultimately not *your* strength; it's *his* strength. And you'll be revived. You will come back to life. You can be the man you were created to be. You can make a difference. You can live righteously. You can be a man of integrity.

Remember, it's only when you let your need drive you to God that he can meet your deepest need.

Do you have the courage to return to God in humility? If you can be honest with yourself, if you can admit that you've been letting your emotions drive you—your anger, your pride, even your despair—and then acknowledge that you want God's Spirit to lead you from now on, he'll meet you where you are.

If you feel empty, low, or defeated, God wants to revive your strength. God wants to renew your purpose, to give you a battle worth fighting for. You are created to fight and win battles that benefit others, not just yourself. You're called to be on the front lines, pushing back the enemy, glorifying your King.

Fighting for what's right is not just what you do. It's who you are. You are a warrior, his warrior, battling for his divine cause.

God wants to give you a cause greater than yourself. Then, once you love something enough that you're willing to die for it, you'll be set free to live. Your emotions will no longer be steering the ship. God's Spirit will become the guiding force for your life.

Consider one example of what happens when we're Spirit-led and not emotion-driven. In 1873, two Christian preachers were talking about a conference they had just attended. Henry Varley said to his new friend Dwight L. Moody, "Moody, the world has yet to see what God will do with a man fully consecrated to him."

We might say it this way today: "The world has yet to see what God will do through one man whose heart is totally surrendered to him."

Those words pierced Moody's soul. Over the following days and weeks, he replayed the truth of them in his mind, contemplating what they meant to him personally. Finally, Moody resolved, "*I* will be that man! If God is looking for a man of integrity, a man of honor and courage and faithfulness, with God's help, *I* will be such a man!"

If you haven't heard that name before, Dwight L. Moody—or D. L. Moody, as he came to be known—went on to become the man that many church historians consider "the greatest evangelist of the nineteenth century."

You can do this. Our twenty-first-century world has yet to see what God will do through a man whose heart is surrendered to him. You could be that man. You have potential that you can't even begin to imagine. Believe me, you don't even know what you're capable of.

So what do you say?

Will you be that man?

//////////////////////////////////////★//////////////////////////////////////

SMALL STEPS
BIG DESTRUCTION

//////////////////////////////////////★//////////////////////////////////////

But until a person can say deeply and honestly, "I am
what I am today because of the choices I made yesterday,"
that person cannot say, "I choose otherwise."
—*Stephen R. Covey*

4.1

SMALL STEPS, BIG DESTRUCTION

Several years ago, I took a group of single Christian adults on a trip to Schlitterbahn (God's water park) in San Antonio. The park features all kinds of waterslides, tube rides, and wave pools. It's a great place for kids as well as adults to stay cool on a scorching Texas summer day.

One of the rides with the longest lines was the boogie board ride. This ride shoots billions of gallons of water at you to mimic an ocean wave, and you ride the wave kneeling on a little board. I was standing there with all these other Christians, watching people ride their boogie boards. At the time, I didn't know that a lot of guys watch this ride because of its reputation for removing women's tops. The water pressure is so intense that it often does more than just topple the rider from her boogie board.

Sure enough, a huge wave came down toward this young woman who was sporting a bikini. When the water crashed onto her bikini top, there was a gasp from the crowd. Unbeknownst to her, the girl had become topless. Instinctively, I looked the other way. All of these Christian guys looked at her, then looked at me, wondering if their pastor was sneaking a peek at the topless girl.

Thankfully, I was looking away (and this light from heaven was shining down upon me).

They were so impressed. "Our pastor didn't look!" they shouted joyfully, repeating the story for months as if I'd crushed the kryptonite offered by a *Maxim* cover model. But it's actually kind of sad that they were so impressed. Why were they impressed? *Because it's not normal to look away.*

Don't get me wrong—I'm no monk. Before I was a Christian, I did more than my share of looking. And after I gave my life to Christ, I still battled the same temptation most red-blooded men face. Temptation still finds me. But I know myself well enough to know my weaknesses and how to protect myself. I've built safeguards into my life. And that includes anticipating situations at water parks that might reveal more than I should see.

Maybe you're thinking, *What's the big deal, Craig? It's only one glance. One moment of private enjoyment isn't going to hurt anyone.* Well, it's a big deal because the things we allow into our minds can lead us to dark places. One step becomes another and then another.

Or maybe you're thinking, *I thought we already covered lust earlier in this book. Here we go again.* Maybe you're one of those guys who doesn't struggle with lust at all. (Though usually such guys struggle with lying, I've found.) But the fact is that lust and sexual temptation are not one-time events. Sexual images, temptations, and pleasures surround us 24/7 in our culture. Not only do most people find no shame in indulging in them, it's expected. If you're a "real" guy, then you're supposed to be a sexual beast, a stud, a leader of the pack, a stallion the ladies can't resist—right?

Wrong.

You're supposed to be a man stronger than his physical urges or emotional responses. You're supposed to be a warrior who's willing to fight for something more important. And that's a battle that's fought one temptation at a time.

Just ask Samson. When we last left our mighty man, he had just turned his heart back to God. He gave God the credit for giving him the strength to kill a thousand Philistines with the jawbone of a donkey, and God miraculously provided water for him to drink. And with Samson's renewed relationship with God, "his strength returned and he revived" (Judg. 15:18–19).

The very next verse is so short it would be easy to read right past it without even realizing its significance. Judges 15:20 says, "Samson led Israel for twenty years in the days of the Philistines."

Just think about what an amazing turnaround a statement like that represents. After all the damage Samson had caused, just one tiny verse encapsulates twenty years of steadfast faithfulness in his life.

Let the power of this sink in for a moment. No matter what you've done (or haven't done), God can still use you as his leader. Even if you've messed up massively and see no hope to lead a God-pleasing life again, with God's help you can win one battle at a time. You can find reconciliation with those you've hurt, restoration where your life is broken, and healing where you've been sick. Like Samson, you can turn the corner onto a new life.

As soon as Samson got back on the right track, God set him in a place of honor and helped him do what he was created to do. In Samson's time, Israel didn't have a king. They used a system of leadership based on righteous judges assigned by God's priests. That's what this verse is referring to; Samson served Israel as a trustworthy judge for twenty years.

If only it had lasted. But it's like they say: old habits die hard. Especially for men.

4.2

★ ONE DAY ★

L et's take a quick look ahead to where Samson's going to end up. He's finally doing well, honoring God with his life and serving God's people. Unfortunately, "as a dog returns to its vomit, so fools repeat their folly" (Prov. 26:11). Gross, I know. But what's even more gross is the destruction that follows our small steps away from God's standard.

Samson slips back into his old habits, and this guy with so much God-given potential starts stacking up one poor decision on top of another again. By the time the consequences of his missteps have run their course, Samson, his eyes gouged out and his arms in chains, is hauled away as a laughingstock in front of his old enemies, the Philistines. He's reduced to being a prisoner, a slave, a once formidable force leashed like a dog.

How could this happen to him? How could a man ordained by God, set apart for greatness—a guy who served God faithfully for twenty years—mess up his life so badly? The answer really shouldn't be all that surprising: Samson didn't ruin his life all at once. He ruined it the same way men have been ruining their lives since the beginning of time.

He ruined it one step at a time.

Think about it. Very few men screw up all at once. They make one bad decision, followed by another compromise, then a lie, on top of another sinful decision. Little by little, they dig a big, sinful hole that feels impossible to climb out of. Let's have a look at where Samson's slow-motion train wreck starts. Remember, we just read that he was having a good twenty-year run. But then *"one day* Samson went to Gaza, where he saw a prostitute. He went in to spend the night with her" (Judg. 16:1, emphasis mine).

Whoa. Really? A whole twenty-year streak and then what? "One day"?

This verse reminds me so much of when King David fell for Bathsheba. That story starts off similarly to this one. Scripture says in 2 Samuel 11:2–3, *"One evening* David got up from his bed and walked around on the roof of the palace. From the roof he saw a woman bathing. The woman was very beautiful, and David sent someone to find out about her" (emphasis mine).

In David's story, it was springtime, "when kings go off to war." Only, King David didn't go off to war. He had someplace he was supposed to be, but basically he decided not to go in to work because the weather was nice. (Have you noticed that being in the wrong place never helps you do the right thing?) David's men are out battling the enemies of his kingdom, bleeding and dying. Meanwhile, back at the palace, David's out for a little evening stroll on his rooftop, where he spots Bathsheba—taking a bath, no less—and he thinks, *Aw, yeah! That's what I'm talking about.*

So how do guys who seem destined for greatness end up on that path to destruction? It's pretty easy, actually. It starts with just one step. One day. One evening. That's all it takes to get the ball rolling. One day you make one bad decision. Then you keep putting one foot in front of the other, and you don't make any course corrections. You keep it a secret. Cover it up. Ignore the warning signs. Each step turns you slightly off the good road you were on, turning you more and more, until inertia pulls you into a downward spiral.

Nine times out of ten, the bad times start when a man goes someplace he's got no business being in the first place.

I'm just going to have a look around.

I'll just kill some time.

I won't stay long; I'm just curious.

Remember when Samson did this twenty years earlier? In Judges 14:1, he "went down to Timnah"—enemy territory. That was when his troubles all began.

This time, we find the decisions that kick off his next harebrained hormonal escapades in Judges 16:1–2. "One day Samson went to Gaza, where he saw a prostitute. He went in to spend the night with her. The people of Gaza were told, 'Samson is here!' So they surrounded the place and lay in wait for him all night at the city gate. They made no move during the night, saying, 'At dawn we'll kill him.'"

Let me ask you a question: when in the history of mankind did it ever end up being a good idea to visit a prostitute? That mistake should be pretty obvious.

But why is it significant that he went to Gaza? Well, Gaza was the headquarters of the Philistines, twenty-five miles away from Samson's hometown of Zorah. Samson was *supposed* to be holding his court, hearing the problems of the Israelites and rendering fair judgments for them. But instead he heads out, right into the heart of Philistine territory, looking for some action. He travels twenty-five miles out of his way to roll the dice on twenty years of faithfulness.

Before you scoff at what a perpetual moron Samson is, don't be so quick to judge. Some men have been known to go to bars, strip clubs, or sketchy massage parlors while they're out of town.

They tell themselves it was just an impulsive, crazy decision while they were traveling for work.

Maybe. But it didn't help that they just happened to have done a little online research to find the hot spots in the cities they'd be visiting. Or the guy who just happens to take the long way home, which just happens to take him by the porn shop on the other side of town. Big shocker, then, when he finds himself stopping.

Sometimes we go to great lengths to try to fool ourselves, working hard to deny that we're risking everything for a few moments of pleasure.

Why would *anyone* do something so obscene and for so little payoff? That's a great question. We should probably take a poll and ask the guys around us. Because the sad truth is, men still do it today, every single day. We'll see some guy who seems to have a good marriage, a successful ministry, integrity to spare, and a booming career, and he risks everything for a sexual hit, a quick high. It's just not worth it. Why do it?

And yet men do it all the time.

////////////////////////// ★ //////////////////////////

STEP BY STEP

////////////////////////// ★ //////////////////////////

Since I'm a pastor, many people think I work only one day a
week. (Although, since our church has services on both Saturdays and Sundays, I guess I work two days a week.) And since
I don't have anything to do during the rest of the week besides
watch my Bible hover above my desk, sometimes I like to pass the
time by sitting around and asking myself things like, *I wonder
how many steps a person would have to take to walk twenty-five miles.*

So I did a little research, and it turns out that to walk
twenty-five miles — the distance Samson traveled from Zorah
to Gaza — would take about 56,250 steps. Now, remember: most
men don't ruin their lives all at once; they ruin them one step at
a time. In Samson's case, he had 56,250 opportunities to change
his mind, turn around, and just go back home. Every single step
he took toward Gaza, he could have said to himself, *This is asinine, Samson. This is so dangerous. What are you doing, man?*

But of course, he didn't.

No man *plans* to ruin his life. I've never met even just one guy
who said, "You know what? My ten-year goal is to become a sex
addict. I want to get so locked into my own little fantasy world
of pornographic lust that it consumes my waking thoughts. I
want to get myself to the point where I can't have any kind of

legitimate, meaningful, intimate relationships because the only way I can ever see any woman is as some kind of sexual object."

That's never what happens. Here's how it really goes down: A guy is just on the computer or playing on his phone, minding his own business, doing his work, maybe researching how many steps it takes to get from Zorah to Gaza, when some ad with a picture of a hot babe suddenly appears at the edge of some web page. He thinks to himself, *Hmm. Well, isn't that interesting? Free—really? No harm in checking it out.*

Click. Now he's on some website that was the farthest thing from his mind just ten seconds ago. But now, on this page, there's another "interesting" thing to click on, something a bit more provocative. Click. He feels that familiar rush. His heart beats faster. He forgets about his wife, his children, his faith. Then, almost like he's on autopilot, it turns into *click, click, click, click, click, click, click, click.* Over time, he ends up in a bad place. And he didn't get there all at once; he got there one step at a time.

I've never met a guy who said, "You know what would be cool, Craig? I can't think of any goal more worthy than to have to file for bankruptcy one day." It doesn't happen like that. He sees some other guy with more than he has and thinks, *Why couldn't that be me?*

Step.

He wants the car, the house, the golf clubs. And the loan terms make it all seem so affordable.

Step.

But then once he starts falling a little behind on payments, he starts scrambling around for solutions. Step. Maybe some gambling, maybe some multilevel marketing scheme. Maybe a cash loan on his credit card to cover another bill. Step, step, step. *All I need is one big score to get back on track.* This guy who couldn't even balance his checkbook starts a business.

Step by step –

Step, step, step, and one day he wakes up in big trouble.

I've never met a guy who said, "I have a really great marriage. My kids love me, and everything seems to be going really well. I think I'll blow it all with an affair." It's not like he was just walking down the street one day and he slipped and fell, and when he landed he was on top of a naked woman on a bed in some hotel room.

No, it starts with one step. An attractive coworker touches him on the arm, just once, and he thinks, *What? Is there something there? She* is *pretty cute.*

Step.

Another time, he says something kind of flirty. Step. She responds! Step. He thinks about her at night. Step. He puts on an extra squirt of cologne just in case he gets close to her. Step. He sends her a text. Step. He puts his hand on her back one time when they're looking at a project together on her computer. Step. They innocently go to lunch one time. Step. One thing leads to another, until they both find themselves emotionally involved. And entangled.

Step, step, step. His marriage and family life are blown apart in a nuclear explosion of pain and betrayal.

A man doesn't ruin his life all at once.

He does it one step at a time.

DON'T TAUNT
THE ENEMY

Samson took three small steps that started the spiral that led to his big destruction. Truthfully, most men who wander away from God and into trouble take these same steps. The first was that he taunted his enemy. Remember that in Judges 16:1–2, Samson had gone to visit a, *ahem*, "user friendly" woman (a prostitute). And when the Philistines learned he was there, several of them plotted to ambush him at dawn. But, verse 3 says, "Samson lay there only until the middle of the night. Then he got up and took hold of the doors of the city gate, together with the two posts, and tore them loose, bar and all. He lifted them to his shoulders and carried them to the top of the hill that faces Hebron."

So instead of spending the whole night with the prostitute, Samson slipped out quietly and under the cover of night tore the doors off the city gates and hauled them away. These were no hollow-core doors. One commentary I read estimates that together these doors would have weighed about seven hundred pounds. Maybe seven hundred pounds doesn't seem like that much to you. (That's about what I deadlift. And by deadlift I mean that's the last thing I lift before I die.) But it is. A lot.

When Samson used his supernatural strength to tear down the Philistines' massive doors and carry them off, he essentially was giving them the middle finger. Those huge doors were how they locked down the city walls at night; they were symbols of their security. By taking them, Samson was saying, "You think you're safe? Your rickety doors can't save you from me."

He was taunting his enemies.

The problem with taunting your enemies is that you often underestimate them, conveniently ignoring this reality: enemies are dangerous. The truth is we have a spiritual enemy, Satan, whose sole mission (as we saw before) is to "steal and kill and destroy" everything that matters to the heart of God (John 10:10). And he has thousands of years of experience convincing guys just like you and me to cave in. And *you're* going to be the one who finally outsmarts him at his own game? Seriously? That's your plan?

That's why Scripture warns us in 1 Peter 5:8, "Be alert and of sober mind. Your enemy the devil prowls around like a roaring lion looking for someone to devour." This is serious business, guys. Satan doesn't just want to wound you, to hurt you; he wants to destroy you, to devour you.

And in case you weren't paying attention earlier, what biological family does the lion belong to? That's right: the *cat* family! Cat, lion, Satan—do you see a pattern here? This may be a complete aside, but I do want to be clear that although I tease a lot about cats, these are just jokes. My family has two cats. While it's true that I don't particularly like cats, my kids *love* cats. And I love my kids just a little more than I dislike cats, so we have two of them, Freddy and Binky. Freddy is decent enough as cats go, I guess. But Binky is unquestionably a bad cat. So I taunt my enemy Binky sometimes.

Just so you'll know that I'm not a horrible guy, let me tell you about Binky. When Binky was a kitten, he was hit by a car, so now he has only three legs (two in the back and one in the front). When the accident happened, with compassion that can come only from God on high, I paid eight hundred dollars for surgery after surgery after surgery for this stupid cat. While he's fine and healthy now, he has only three legs, so I call him Tripod.

Binky the Tripod likes to work his way up onto the kitchen counters. But because that's where we prepare our food, that's not okay with me. It's disgusting. I don't want cat butt on my counters. Although I never would hit a defenseless animal, it's not beneath me to startle one. I head-fake Binky, jolting my head at his and saying, "Boo!" That's always been a safe taunt because, with only three legs, he can't swipe at me. If he did, he'd fall.

Once, Binky was on the counter again, antagonizing me, because he knows good and well he's not supposed to be up there. I sneaked up alongside him and gave him my head-fake with a "boo!" Since he couldn't swipe at me, while I was still in close, he lunged forward and bit my nose! Men, do *not* underestimate your enemy. (Sorry about digressing. I just had to tell someone about my battle scar and writing about it is cheaper than counseling.)

I know a lot of men who have committed themselves to honor God by remaining sexually pure. But even among those guys, I've met many who just constantly take risks, dancing with temptation again and again. You commit to wait to have sex until you're married. Then your girlfriend comes over to your apartment, and you hang out there, alone, "talking." On the bed. Until the wee hours of the morning. What are you thinking? It's just dangerous.

Don't underestimate your enemy.

Let's say you're married and you go away on a business trip.

Everybody else is heading out for drinks after work, and you think, *Sure, I can handle this. No big deal.* So you go out and have a drink. And you're laughing with your new friends and having a good time. Then one drink leads to two, which spills into three, which sloshes into four, and then suddenly you're thinking, *Man! Where did all these women come from? I didn't see them come in.* You start thinking you're good looking and funny. You start thinking you've still got it (even if you never had it in the first place).

You're just taunting your enemy. Even worse, you're underestimating him.

Or maybe you don't have any money, so you think, *What's something free we could do? Hey, I know! Let's go walk around a car lot and "just look around."* What are you doing? You're taunting the enemy. Don't underestimate the finance department.

Perhaps you're hanging out with some guys who are not likely to go to your small group Bible study—ever. They cuss. They cheat. They lie. They steal. And you think, *I'll be a witness to them, show them God's love.* But instead of bringing them up, you know they're actually bringing you down. You think it's not affecting you, but deep down you know your spiritual light has already started to dim.

A lot of you are probably thinking, *Well, that's all well and good, Craig. But that's not me. You're talking to other guys.* If that's true, then *this* is for you: "If you think you are standing firm, be careful that you don't fall!" (1 Cor. 10:12).

Taunting his enemy was only the first of Samson's major mistakes. He also made two other missteps.

4.5

HEY THERE, DELILAH

The first time we saw Samson do something wrong was when he went down to Timnah, where he fell for a Philistine woman. Whether or not you've dedicated your life to God as a Nazirite, you shouldn't go after women who worship false gods. It's just never a good idea. Well, guess who's up to his old tricks? Judges 16:4 tells us, "Some time later, [Samson] fell in love with a woman in the Valley of Sorek whose name was Delilah."

"Some time later" means after he had been with the prostitute and then torn off Gaza's front doors—just to be sure he got himself back on the Philistines' radar. And then, of course, he fell in love with Delilah. I can't help wondering what he was thinking. Maybe, *You know, I haven't had very good luck with these Philistine chicks. Maybe the third time's the charm.*

The truth is, as so many men do, Samson was simply rationalizing his sin. Some guys justify their sin based on how "clean" the rest of their life is: *This is my one vice. I'm a good guy. I don't do anything else bad.* Other men justify it as something private: *What I do is nobody else's business anyway. It's my life. I can do what I want. I don't care what other people think.* A lot of guys let themselves off the hook with this lie: *If nobody knows, what's the big deal? What I'm doing isn't hurting anybody. Besides, I'm just looking at the menu. I'm not gonna order anything.*

Probably most of us simply blame our sin on somebody else: *If my own woman would just do a little more with me, I wouldn't even need this. As it is, these little "supplements" are the only way I can make it through the stress of my day.* No matter what angle we use, most of us men are masters at rationalizing the same old sin — just like Samson.

Let's look at what happens next in verse 5: "The rulers of the Philistines went to [Delilah] and said, 'See if you can lure [Samson] into showing you the secret of his great strength and how we can overpower him so we may tie him up and subdue him. Each one of us will give you eleven hundred shekels of silver.'"

They bribed her. They offered her cash to give him up. You should read this yourself in Judges 16:6 – 14, but I'll summarize it for you.

The next time they're alone together, Delilah tells Samson, "Tell me the secret of your great strength."

Samson lies to her. "Well, if you tie me up with seven bowstrings, I'll be just as weak as any other man." (In another version of the Bible, he says "thongs," but thongs remind me of flip-flops or ... something else. I'm sticking with bowstrings.)

After Samson falls asleep, she ties him up with bowstrings and says, "Samson, the Philistines are upon you!"

He easily breaks free and escapes, so the next time they're together, she says, "You lied to me. Tell me, what's your secret, really?"

He lies again. "Brand new ropes. If you tie me up with new ropes, I'll be as weak as any other man."

Again he falls asleep. This time she ties him up with brand new ropes, then says, "Samson, the Philistines are upon you!"

And again he breaks free and escapes.

The next time he comes to see her, she won't let it go. "Come on! You lied to me. Tell me what the real thing is."

He gets closer to telling her the truth this time. He says, "It's my hair. If you weave the braids from my hair into the fabric on a loom and lock them with the pin, I'll be as weak as any man."

Again she tries what he said, and again she cries out, "Samson, the Philistines are upon you!"

And again he has no trouble escaping.

Finally, the next time Samson and Delilah are together, she's had enough. She says, "How can you say, 'I love you,' when you won't confide in me? This is the third time you have made a fool of me and haven't told me the secret of your great strength.' *With such nagging she prodded him day after day until he was sick to death of it*" (vv. 15–16, emphasis mine). Okay, do I really need to say anything here? Did you really think that you're the first guy who's ever felt like your wife just won't let it go? (And ladies, if you're still reading this, I'm not justifying any of Samson's actions here, but I'm just saying that nagging is never the way to encourage your man.)

What's interesting about this failure of Samson's is we kind of have to assume that by this time, he must have realized what Delilah was up to. Every time he told her the "secret" of his strength, he awoke tied up in just the way he had told her to. But even though she kept trying to give him up to the Philistines, he kept returning to her. Doesn't that say so much about how men's minds work? Even in the face of great danger, of near-certain disaster, we keep going back to something just because it feels good. We can always justify the things we want.

Samson was a warrior strong enough to kill a thousand men. He was strong enough to rip a lion apart with his bare hands.

He was strong enough to pull seven-hundred-pound doors from their posts and carry them off. But in the end, he wasn't strong enough to lead a woman. That's your warning in a nutshell, gentlemen. Don't dare be strong just in business or at your job. Don't dare be strong just in your hobbies or at some sport. Don't dare settle for being strong just physically. Focus your strength on leading those around you into righteousness. A lot of men are strong in all kinds of ways, but they leave the leadership to others.

Don't let that be you.

Don't settle for being strong at what doesn't last and weak at what does. Tap into the warrior within. Don't fight just the meaningless battles. Fight for what matters most. And fight for your life.

Let's look at where things start coming apart: "So he told her everything. 'No razor has ever been used on my head,' he said, 'because I have been a Nazirite dedicated to God from my mother's womb. If my head were shaved, my strength would leave me, and I would become as weak as any other man'" (v. 17).

Remember Samson's three Nazirite vows:

1. Don't get drunk.
2. Don't touch anything unclean.
3. Don't get your hair cut.

One thing I really like about this verse is how Samson refers to the fact that he was set apart to God since birth. It's almost as if he remembers, just for a moment, who he was created to be.

What about you? Can you still remember the man you were created to be? Do you remember those moments when you were just a boy, reveling in the joy of pretending you were one of your heroes? That's not just childish, make-believe stuff. Even as adults, our heroes inspire us because they fan the flame that God ignited within us. They remind us of the hero within ourselves.

Sadly, just glimpsing that truth isn't enough by itself. Without action, without choosing your next step differently, the outcome is inevitable. Verse 19: "After putting him to sleep on her lap, she called for someone to shave off the seven braids of his hair, and so began to subdue him. And his strength left him."

I wonder how many men out of disobedience to God try to do battle every single day in their own strength. It would be so easy to tap into the power of God. All it takes is returning to the vows you once made. But just like Samson, we don't mess up our lives all at once. We do it one step at a time. We doom ourselves when we taunt the enemy, when we rationalize our sin, and then when we assume that our disobedience isn't going to cost us anything. We forget that our sin always takes us farther than we want to go and costs us more than we want to pay.

HIDDEN COSTS

true

Have you ever done something you knew you shouldn't, something you weren't supposed to do, and then *nothing bad happened?* A lot of men today seem to believe they can just keep getting away with doing the same thing over and over. Samson kept chasing forbidden women. Sure, he suffered some emotional consequences, but it never cost him the thing he seemed to care about most, the thing he relied on: his strength.

Until Judges 16:20. Delilah called out, "'Samson, the Philistines are upon you!' He awoke from his sleep and thought, 'I'll go out as before and shake myself free.' But he did not know that the LORD had left him."

Just as before, Samson didn't think that his disobedience was going to cost him. But he didn't know that things had changed. Take this as another warning for us: You may have gotten away with it once. You even may have gotten away with it more than once. Nobody ever caught you. No one has held you accountable. But mark my words, the day is coming when the truth will come out.

And when it does, you might go back to your wife one more time, thinking you're going to sweet-talk your way out of trouble, just like you always have, but instead she's going to say, "I've had enough of your games. There won't be another time. I'm leaving."

Or you're going to go home to your kids and say, "I'm sorry, guys. I just got busy at work and forgot. We'll go next time. I promise!" But your kids are going to say, "Whatever, Dad. I don't even care anymore. I'm sick of wasting my time waiting for you to keep your promises. I don't believe anything you say."

Or you're going to go to your boss and say, "Sorry, the leads just weren't there this month. But I have some ideas. I'm going to try out some new things, and next month is going to be different." But your boss is going to say, "No. Enough! You always have 'new ideas.' And then you just do the same things again. You've been cutting corners. You've exaggerated your leads. You've lied too many times for me to take you seriously. We're done here. Come with me to Human Resources."

Just like Samson, we keep thinking, *I'll just do what I did last time. I'll shake myself free.* But our sins always overtake us eventually, overpowering us. Your sin *will* find you out. And then, you'll face your own verse 21: "Then the Philistines seized [Samson], gouged out his eyes and took him down to Gaza. Binding him with bronze shackles, they set him to grinding grain in the prison."

How does a man with so much God-given potential end up in such an awful place? He didn't do it all at once. He did it one step at a time.

Which brings us to your moment of truth: where are you stepping away from God? Please slow down for a minute and think about the answer to this question. This could be one of the most important moments of your life. Whether you're on step number one or step number 56,249, where are you stepping away from God?

It could be something simple, like you're a Christian, but you're not spending time in God's Word. Or you're a Christian, but you're not spending time in prayer. Your hair is still long.

You're still going to church. You have the outward signs that you're following God. But inside, your heart has drifted from him.

It could be lust: "I want it. I've got to have it." Maybe you've been taking baby steps toward some pornographic snare. It could be entitlement: "I deserve it." Or it could be pride: "I can handle it."

It could be anger. You're frustrated and you have a short fuse. You're mad at yourself, but you take it out on everyone else. One small thing can launch you into one big rage.

It could be apathy and passive living. You're aggressive in some areas of your life, but you're not leading in areas where you know you should be. You promise you'll do something, but your promises don't mean much these days.

It could be greed. You love the things of this world, and you want more. You want to keep up with the Kardashians — and you don't even like the Kardashians. Maybe you're financially irresponsible, even sinful. The list of possibilities really is endless. It just depends on you.

Be courageous, and be honest: where are you stepping away from God?

Because you are only as strong as you are honest.

This whole book has been building to this moment. Are you stepping away from God in any way? Are you on step number one? Or step number 56,249? Or somewhere in between? No matter how many steps you've already taken, there's a simple and profound solution. It's so basic, so commonsensical, that if you're not paying attention, you just might miss it: turn around.

That's it. Turn around. Go the other way! It's not too late. It really is that simple. Fight the momentum of moving toward sin and go the other direction. And when you turn around, who will be right there waiting for you? Your God. Because he is that good.

The last verse in this particular chapter of Samson's life is me the most exciting, grace-filled verse in this entire story. What is the outward symbol of Samson's inward devotion to God? His hair. But he has lost it to his enemies. He's been subdued, publicly ashamed, and dragged away to prison. His baldness announces to everyone who sees him, "I have disobeyed God." But God is merciful. This one verse, verse 22, captures God's love and grace: "But the hair on his head began to grow again."

Even though Samson has disobeyed God and is now living with the consequences, God's grace is sufficient for him. God, the ultimate warrior, sends a message to Samson: "The fight is not over. That which gives you strength will grow again!"

So what's it going to be? More secrets? More fear? More hiding? Or are you finally going to tell the truth? If you're going the wrong way, stop. Stop now. Fall on your knees and fight like a man. Cry out to God. Ask him to forgive you. Embrace his grace. Receive his forgiveness. Get up. Turn around. And walk the other way.

If you've stepped away, whether one step or thousands, turn around. It's not too late. God's grace is enough for you. How? First John 1:9–10 tells us, "If we confess our sins, he is faithful and just and will forgive us our sins and purify us from all unrighteousness. If we claim we have not sinned, we make him out to be a liar and his word is not in us." That means when we confess to God, when we admit what we've done wrong, we have his forgiveness. It costs us nothing but our honesty and courage.

But that's only part of the equation of returning to the path we need to be on. Confessing to God gets us forgiveness, but not necessarily healing. James 5:16 tells us how we can do that: "Confess your sins to each other and pray for each other so that you may be healed." You don't just need to confess to God; you also need to confess to the people who matter, the people who have been affected by your sins. (You know who they are.) It may be your spouse, your friends, your children, your coworkers, or your teammates. Share the true you with them, and ask for their forgiveness. Ask them to pray for you. It will be painful, sure, both for you and for them, but it's time for you to turn.

WEAPONS OF WAR

Once you've turned around, you're going to have to fight. The good news, though, is that God equips every warrior for the battle before him. In 2 Corinthians 10:3–4, here's how the Bible describes those weapons: "For though we live in the world, we do not wage war as the world does. The weapons we fight with are not the weapons of the world. On the contrary, they have divine power to demolish strongholds." Ephesians 6:12 describes the real war: "Our struggle is not against flesh and blood, but against the rulers, against the authorities, against the powers of this dark world and against the spiritual forces of evil in the heavenly realms."

Your enemy hates your guts. Do you get that? He despises you. Why? Because he hates everything that matters to God, and nothing matters more to God than you. Your enemy is a worthy adversary. His name is Satan. The Bible calls him the father of lies. He's the great deceiver. And he wants to destroy you.

Do you realize Satan has been studying humankind for thousands of years? Our weaknesses. *Your* weaknesses. He designs devices and sets up schemes to hurt you and the people you love. To steal from you, to destroy you, and ultimately to kill you.

Men, if another man was trying to hurt your family, what

/ould you do? You'd take him out. Wouldn't you? You would unload on anyone who tried to harm those you love.

It's time to fight. The stakes couldn't be higher. Defend yourself. Fight back. Don't just sit there. Throw a punch. And fight dirty. We don't fight with the weapons of this world; we fight with the weapon of God's Word.

Ephesians 6 says we must put on the full armor of God. Why? Because we're at war. Christianity's not a playground. It's a battleground.

Put on your helmet of salvation, the mind of Christ. We are protected because we are right with God through Christ.

Put on your breastplate of righteousness. We are righteous not because of anything we can do but because of what Christ has already done.

Pick up your shield of faith. The accuser knows how to take you down: "You're not good enough. You'll never measure up. You can't afford another false start. You don't have what it takes. Loser." Don't listen to the deceiver. Believe what God says about you. You are who he says you are. You are a spiritual warrior. Believe it.

Put on your belt of truth. Don't buy into the lies: temptation, lust, pride, riches. Stand courageously on God's truth.

Put on your boots, the gospel of peace. Plant your feet firmly and stand. When you've done everything else you can do, stand.

God calls you to stand. Your enemy wants you to fall. So as God's warrior, there are only two acceptable actions. You're either standing or you're getting back up. Even if Satan trips you, you're not down forever. Get back up. Never stay down.

But don't just defend yourself. Advance. Use what the Bible calls the sword of the Spirit, the Word of God. This, our greatest weapon, is lethal, sharp, alive, and active. Using your faith, apply God's Word to your life and watch him fight on your behalf.

Finally, pray. Remember, the strongest man is not the one who lifts the most weight but the one with the most faith.

Instead of taking step after mindless step toward your own destruction, it's time you learned to fight. Jesus said there's a time to "turn the other cheek." Ecclesiastes says there's not only a time for peace but also a time for war. I believe the church has too often stripped men of permission to stand up for themselves, to draw a line in the sand and say, "Satan, if you step across this line, I'm fighting back." While I'm not advocating violence, as you have already seen, I firmly believe that sometimes God gives us permission to fight.

Let me illustrate with something that happened almost a decade ago. Our family was at a party at someone else's house, and this four-year-old started picking on my son Sam, who was about three at the time. The other boy, while his dad and I were standing right there, walked up to Sam and pushed him down. Sam got up, startled, and looked at me with *What do I do?* in his eyes. I said, "Just shake it off, Sam."

The kid pushed him down harder a second time, right in front of me and his own dad. Sam started to cry. He looked to me again. I said, "Just shake it off."

I glared at his father, thinking, *Aren't you going to do something about your bully son?* Then the kid pushed Sam down *again*. I glared harder at his dad. He said, "Boys will be boys," and kind of laughed it off.

Sam was crying. I said, "Sam, just go in the other room. Just walk away. Walk away." Sam sniffled, turned, and obediently started to walk away. The four-year-old ran up behind Sam and pushed him down, head first, as he was trying to walk away. I could hardly believe what was happening.

I crouched down to Sam's height and said, "Sam, look at me." He looked up at me through his tears. I said firmly, "Take him."

Sam's whole demeanor changed. Tears still in his eyes, he charged, and he tackled the bigger boy. When Sam made contact, the two went airborne. They crashed onto the floor. The other boy scrambled up and ran to his mom, who was standing nearby.

I shrugged at his dad and said, "Oh well. Boys will be boys."

If this story offends you, understand that this is serious business. When we strip men of permission to fight back at the appropriate time, we emasculate them. We stifle the spirit of the warrior that God placed within them, the spirit that yearns to fight for what's right. When men feel stripped of power, it's that much easier to give in to temptation. If they've never learned to fight, then it's hard to know how to fight the deadliest enemy of all.

On September 11, 2001, four airplanes went down, in New York, in Washington, and in Pennsylvania. I was actually on an airplane when the attacks began. Todd Beamer was on one too. He did what I hope I would do, what I hope my son would do. An enemy was on his plane, using strength to harm innocent people. After secretly phoning people on the ground, Todd learned that other evil men were flying planes into buildings to kill innocent people.

Realizing that these men planned to do the same with his plane, Todd wouldn't — Todd *couldn't* — stand for it. Here was a man with the heart of a warrior. It was time. He drew a line in the sand and said, "Let's roll." I don't know exactly what happened on that plane. But one man with a cause greater than his own life made a stand: "I won't let you kill innocent people. I will take you down, take this plane down. If I go down with it, so be it. I'll give my life to save others." That is the heart of a warrior.

We must be consumed by God's truth enough to say, "We'll fight for the cause of Christ. We won't back down. We won't surrender." And when you fight for the cause God gives you, you never fight without his strength. Deuteronomy 20:3–4 says, "Hear, Israel: Today you are going into battle against your enemies. Do not be fainthearted or afraid; do not panic or be terrified by them. For the LORD your God is the one who goes with you to fight for you against your enemies to give you victory."

What battle are you facing? Give it a name.

Marriage crumbling? Draw your sword. Fight. Don't surrender. It's a cause that's beyond yourself.

Kids turning away from God? Pray them back to God. Use God's weapons.

Drowning financially? Fight. Discipline yourself to start winning small battles.

Surrounded on every side by your sin? Unleash the warrior's heart inside of you. Fight. Romans 8:37 says we are "more than conquerors through [Christ] who loved us." We overcome, Revelation tells us, by the blood of the Lamb and by the words of our testimonies. Our strength is not our own. We can do all things through Christ who strengthens us.

You have the heart of a warrior. Nothing can distract you. People cannot disillusion you. Critics cannot derail you. Demons cannot stop you.

You are a man. God gave you a cause to inspire you. Honor it. God gave you weapons to fight for it. Face your fear. Tell the truth. Fight, and fight to win. You're ready, you have permission, and you're not alone. It's time to quit walking blindly through your life falling into the traps of your enemy.

It's time to turn around and fight for your life.

FAILING FORWARD

Failures are finger posts on the road to achievement.

—*C. S. Lewis*

//////////////////////////////// ★ ////////////////////////////////

FAILING FORWARD

//////////////////////////////// ★ ////////////////////////////////

Ihave two sons, two young warriors — Sam (whom you've heard about) and Stephen. (We call Sam "Cruncher" because he crunches everything. We call Stephen "Bookie" because his older brother called him "Booby" when he was a baby, and we found that unacceptable. Booby is not a good name for a warrior. You understand.) Helping Cruncher and Bookie become the warriors God wants them to be has not been without its challenges.

Years ago, late in the springtime, several of us were playing together outside. I put Sam (who was two years old) on a scooter, and I taught him to do something that I shouldn't have. Starting out at the top of our driveway, I demonstrated how to coast down, down, faster and faster, all the way to the bottom. I did it a couple of times to show him how.

Then he tried it, and he was doing great. (*A chip off the old block*, I thought proudly.) But what began as the time of his life ended abruptly in a broken femur. I still remember that horrible sound. That *crack!* seemed to echo infinitely, and Sam shrieked in agony. He endured incredible pain, and my foolish fathering cost him six weeks in a full-body cast, and it was another two weeks after that before he could walk again.

The whole event was, to say the least, traumatic. While we

were at the hospital, Amy told me, "I want you to throw that scooter away. Burn it. I don't ever want to see it again as long as I live." My girls were afraid of the scooter because of "what it had done to Sam." *Bad scooter. Bad! We hate scooters!* Whenever my wife or kids walked through the garage, they gave the cursed instrument of evil a wide berth so it wouldn't attack them and break their legs. Everyone—especially Sam—wanted me to get rid of it.

I declined.

As terrible as I felt for teaching Sam something that ended up hurting him, I knew we weren't done with the scooter. I knew that one day my mighty warrior Sam would have to face his fear. When the horse throws you, you have to get back in the saddle. You can't just lie on the ground and embrace your fear of horses. My son was going to have to ride that scooter again.

You probably won't be surprised to hear that Amy disagreed. Emphatically. It made for many spirited conversations about parenting and the differences between boys and girls, fathers and mothers, women and warriors. I didn't exactly win, but the scooter remained in our garage.

A few months later, once Sam was all put back together again, I casually asked him from time to time, "Sam, are you ready to ride the scooter again?" And every time I asked him, he cried and ran away from me. "No, Daddy! That scooter broke my leg!"

After awhile I eased up. "Well, you just tell Daddy when you're ready again." Weeks passed. Months. Finally, I had forgotten about it, put it out of my mind. The scooter continued to gather dust in our garage behind the skeleton of someone's bicycle and our old leaf blower.

One day I was outside playing ball with several of the kids. Sam approached me, very serious, and said, "Daddy, I'm weady."

"You're ready for what, Sam?" I wondered if I'd forgotten to take him somewhere—a doctor's appointment or a friend's house.

"I'm weady to wide the cootuh."

My jaw dropped, and I stared at my little man, wide-eyed. When I regained my composure, I closed my mouth and nodded. I headed for the garage. The girls bolted, yelling, "We're gonna tell Mom!" We had to act fast. Sam took hold of the scooter handles. As he headed toward the top of the driveway, he started first to cry, then to shake. I put my hand on his and said, "Buddy, look, you don't have to do this today."

He looked up at me through his tears and said something I'll remember for the rest of my life: "No, Daddy. I *have* to ride it. Today."

And so he got on. And he was crying. And then I was crying. And my girls were off somewhere tattling. Through our tears, I took this little warrior on just a little circle, a very safe ride. He jumped off, and though he had managed to stop shaking, now he was sobbing. "Daddy! I did it! I did it! Daddy! Did you see me?"

"Yeah, son! You did it. *You did it.*" The little warrior rode again. He *had* to. It's integral to the way he was made. God didn't make us to be warriors so that we'd be perfect; he made us to be warriors so that we'd fight our fears, learn from our mistakes, and live to fight another day.

THE BLIND SIDE

My son Sam learned something fundamental from getting
on his scooter again, something that took Samson much
longer to grasp. Much of the tragedy of Samson's story is his
failure to be all that he might have been if he'd just been willing
to learn from his mistakes the first time.

For me, Samson remains one of the most frustrating charac-
ters in the Bible. God set him apart from birth, even giving him
supernatural strength to fulfill his calling to lead in the process
of delivering the Israelites from the oppressive rule of the Philistines. But just like so many of us, even with a divine calling and
extraordinary power, Samson somehow managed constantly to
mess things up.

He was an incredibly strong man with a dangerously weak
will. He broke his vows to God, chased forbidden women who
worshiped idols, touched things he wasn't supposed to touch,
drank things he wasn't supposed to drink, and ended up with a
really bad haircut.

His mistakes finally caught up with him, though, and things
weren't looking so good for Samson anymore. He was supposed
to be defeating God's enemies, but ended up losing more than
just his dignity. Of course, he was reduced to normal human

strength when he lost his hair. As if that wasn't enough, the Bible says the Philistines "gouged out his eyes." Most commentaries seem to agree that that means they burned out his eyeballs with fire, scraping out whatever remained. (Ouch — talk about getting blindsided.) Then they shackled him and set him to work grinding grain in a prison. They fastened him to a large wooden turnstile and forced him to walk in circles day after day, like an ox turning a heavy grinding stone. (Think of a supersized caged hamster on the wheel.) It's a good bet his jailers and the other prisoners constantly mocked him, calling him names and throwing things at him, spitting on him, even whipping him. The labor would have been tough enough by itself, but the mind games would have compounded that pain. It would be hard to find yourself lower than where Samson ended up.

An even worse pain for Samson was probably the spiritual agony of having to acknowledge his failure. What would it be like to realize that you had wasted the years God gave you? That you'd wasted the gifts he gave you? You did things you can't undo. You're ashamed of your actions. You've hurt the people you love. And you didn't do what God created you to do. As men, we take that kind of failure personally.

Maybe it's because we should.

Generally speaking, men and women find their value in different ways. Women typically draw their value from their relationships. And because women measure themselves by the quality of their relationships, they're constantly checking in with their friends:

"We're friends, right?"

"I just really need a hug."

"Can we get together soon and just talk?"

"I texted you over ten minutes ago. Haven't heard back.
Kind of freaking out here. Did I say something to
offend you? Please text me back. Just need to know
we're okay."

Everything is relational for women—even going to the bathroom. Why can't a woman just go to the bathroom alone? Why
is it that when one woman goes to the bathroom, they *all* have to
go? It's like it would be rude for a woman to go to the bathroom
without asking another woman to go.

"I'm going to the bathroom. You want to go with me?"

"Sure!"

"Hey, look! There's somebody we know over there at that
other table. Let's take her too!"

"Definitely!" *(waving)* "Yoo hoo!"

Then two hours later they come back arm in arm. What happens in there? Are they opining about why the Bachelor should
have stayed with the *other* girl? Is there a fashion show and panel
discussion on makeup tips? Don't bother asking; they're sworn
to secrecy.

Men like to be liked, but it's not *everything* for us. Most of our
value doesn't come from relationships; it comes from accomplish-
ments: *How do I measure up? Did I do well? Did I win?*

Our relationships do matter to us, just not in the same ways
women's matter to them. No guy would ever say to his fellas,
"Hey, let's all go to the bathroom together!" If he did, he might
have a bloody nose to attend to when he got to the bathroom—
by himself. If guys ever do happen to end up in the bathroom at
the same time, there's a well-understood protocol. I don't think
these rules are written down anywhere, but every guy knows
them. One is that it's okay to speak to each other, but you have to
keep conversation to a minimum.

"Man, that water is cooold."

"Yeah. And deep."

You also *never, ever* make eye contact. You look straight ahead at the wall in front of you. It's *not* okay to turn your head and face another guy when he's taking care of his business. Even more important, you never—under any circumstances—look over and down.

Now that we've thoroughly reviewed the basics of bathroom behavior, let's explore one of the deeper dynamics of the male psyche—if such a thing exists. In relationships, it's more important to a man to be respected than to be liked. That's why men take failure so personally. When we fail, it often feels like we may never recover. During the years that I've been a pastor, I've talked with literally thousands of men, and I am absolutely convinced: a man's greatest fear is failure, and his greatest pain is regret.

Most men don't want to fail even once. We want to measure up and be successful at anything we try. This is why we don't want to play if we don't think we can win. It's typically when we don't live up to our expectations—or to someone else's—that regret sets in: *I wish I had. I should have. Why didn't I?*

5.3

THE RISING COST
OF REGRET

The truth is many of you reading this are going to face some pretty significant regret at some point in your lives. You may one day have to look your wife in the eye—a woman who has been faithful to you for years, giving you children and serving you faithfully throughout your life together—and try to explain to her, "No, you really are enough. That's not what this meant. I promise!" as she cries because she has just caught you looking at porn on the internet. And you'll wish you could undo it.

Or maybe you'll have to try to explain something that's unexplainable, like why you betrayed your marriage vows to chase after some twenty-four-year-old at work. You'll deal with the regret of breaking the heart of the woman who has been by your side through everything, kicking yourself for not kicking out your own Delilah before it was too late.

Or maybe you'll be frustrated every day because you feel like you're trapped in a career that's beneath you. Living paycheck to paycheck, you look around at your friends, and all of them seem to be doing a lot better than you. You'll wish you had tried harder in school, worked harder in your previous jobs, or just not settled for the meaningless one you have now.

Or maybe you'll regret the girl who "got away." You just kept stringing her along, even though you knew she wanted you to propose. She would have been great for you, too, but you just wouldn't commit. You'll think, *Why didn't I treat her better? Like she deserved? I was so selfish. Now I'm alone. How could I have been so stupid?*

Or maybe you'll be that married guy who, even though you were always faithful, let your marriage just skate by, never leading your family to anyplace meaningful. Sure, you remembered your anniversary and everyone's birthdays, you sent your kids to private school, and you took them to football and gymnastics. You even went to church (some of the time). But you never *inspired* them. You never challenged them to live lives that would change the world. You'll kick yourself because it will just be too late.

Or maybe your regret is even simpler than any of those. Maybe you're living out your failure right now, every day. It's not an outward failure; nobody can see it. But inside, you ache from all of those promises you kept making to yourself and to God, but then broke. You regret yesterday. You regret today. And tomorrow's not looking good.

But you need to remember this powerful truth that is just as true for you as it was for Samson: failure is an event, not a person.

Take a minute to let that sink in. There's no way you've failed more than Samson did. Of course he shamed himself, but worse than that, he let down a *nation*. He betrayed his vows and his Lord. His prideful ego and selfish desires caused him to fall again and again.

Still, God wasn't done with him. "The hair on his head began to grow."

If you think God uses only perfect people, then you haven't

read the Bible. Or you haven't been paying attention to the people all around you who are making a difference in this world every day. Only once did God ever use a perfect person. Before then and ever since, for all the rest of us—including Samson, including *you*—he has worked with whatever we have given him.

Notice how God's Word sets the stage for what's going to happen in Judges 16:23–24: "Now the rulers of the Philistines assembled to offer a great sacrifice to Dagon their god and to celebrate, saying, 'Our god has delivered Samson, our enemy, into our hands.' When the people saw him, they praised their god, saying, 'Our god has delivered our enemy into our hands, the one who laid waste our land and multiplied our slain.'"

Sounds like quite the party to me. Once they had Samson safely locked in prison, the important people ("rulers") thought it would be fun to put together a nice worship service to thank their harvest god, Dagon, for helping them finally catch their enemy. Dagon's image was this fish body with the head of a man, sort of a man-fish god. (Sucks to be a Philistine, huh?)

The venue they chose was a kind of temple, which to us probably would look more like a coliseum. Multiple layers of stadium-style seating looked down on the open floor where the action took place. Massive columns at strategic places held up the whole structure. Historians speculate that this structure probably could hold as many as five thousand people.

They praised Dagon for giving them "the one who laid waste our land and multiplied our slain." Samson had devastated their crops, tying one-hundred-fifty pairs of foxes together, attaching lit torches to them, and setting them loose. When they went looking for him afterward, he picked up a donkey's jawbone and clubbed a thousand of them to death. Since we're keeping score, we probably should add to that another thirty fatalities for that dirty little business in Ashkelon I like to call the Dead Men's Wearhouse Incident. While to you and me all of that was just a chapter ago (Judges 15), it was a grudge the Philistines had been carrying for twenty years.

In Judges 16:25, they send for him: "While they were in high spirits, they shouted, 'Bring out Samson to entertain us.' So they called Samson out of the prison, and he performed for them." You couldn't get any lower. In the deepest valley of failure that Samson has ever known, God's enemies parade him out like some kind of freak, utterly humiliated before them.

But Samson's story isn't over yet. They say you can't keep a good man down. Even more so, you can't keep God's man down. Even after hitting rock bottom, the big guy still has a fighting spirit, as we'll see in a moment. But considering how far he'd fallen, it would've been understandable if he'd given up — dead inside, just waiting for his body to catch up. But we always have choices. When we face failure, we can choose between two responses: remorse and repentance.

5.4

JUST WALK AWAY

Unfortunately, remorse is where a lot of men get stuck. The weight of their failures feels crushing, and they can't imagine sinking any lower. They're ready to give up. They know something has to change, but they feel like it's too late. They become paralyzed by their thoughts:

I shouldn't have done that.
I feel awful about what I did.
I'll never make up for all the bad things I've done.

They fret and stew and replay their failures over and over in their heads, an endless loop of shame, bitterness, and regret. They almost feel detached from themselves, watching what they did as if it were a film. They know how it's going to end, but they can't change the channel or fast-forward past their mistakes.

Or sometimes men turn that remorse inward:

I'm no good.
I don't have a future.
Everyone would be better off without me.

These guys aren't accepting responsibility for their actions; they're blaming themselves for being such losers. They assume it's just who they are, as if there's little they could do to change the outcome of their actions. In a sense, they're martyrs of destruction, resigned to their selfish ways and the corresponding collateral damage.

Other times, guys turn the negativity outward, playing the victim and blaming others:

"This wouldn't have happened if you hadn't ..."
"I never asked for this!"
"If people hadn't put so much pressure on me, I wouldn't have collapsed like this."

It's never pretty when men who are supposed to be warriors become whiners. Shifting the responsibility, casting blame on everyone around them, and feeling sorry for themselves, they refuse to own their choices. They refuse to take ownership of their actions and realize that those little steps always lead somewhere.

Samson certainly could have deflected the responsibility for his actions:

"My parents didn't prepare me for what I'd face in life."
"How was I supposed to know Delilah would betray me? I was just trying to trust my woman."
"A man can take only so much. She nagged me until I hit my breaking point. What was I supposed to do?"

But as we'll see at the end of his story, he has a change of heart. He knows he needs God and humbles himself. He's finally willing to relinquish his own life for a larger purpose.

Usually I encourage men to memorize verses from passages we're studying, but I'd probably make an exception in this case. If your main action step is to memorize gems such as, "With such nagging she prodded him day after day until he was sick to death of it," and, "If you had not plowed with my heifer, you would not have solved my riddle," you've probably missed the point. And if you quote one of these to your wife — especially during an argument — don't you dare blame me for whatever happens after that.

Remorse is a common response to failure, but there's a much better one: repentance. Instead of turning inward or deflecting outward, you turn upward. Instead of allowing yourself to get stuck, you stop and then let God move you through it. You drop the guilt, the regret, the anger, and the self-pity and return to the Lord. Repentance means owning up to your mistakes and accepting responsibility:

"This was my fault."
"I've had this coming for a long time now."

But ownership gets you only so far. Repentance requires action. "I didn't do what God entrusted me to do, but now I'm going to turn away from what I did wrong. I'm going to move back toward what I know is right." If your steps are heading in the wrong direction, turn around. That's what repentance is.

Remorse is a feeling based primarily on guilt (a selfish emotion), keeping our attention on the past. Repentance is turning away from that wrong, turning away from the past, and turning our attention to changing our future. Remorse builds an emotional monument to our sin, then stands there gazing at it while we feel bad. Repentance is turning one hundred and eighty degrees *away* from our sin and then walking away from it. With each step, repentance moves farther away from that sin. And it doesn't look back.

5.5

★ TEXT APPEAL ★

All of us have done things we wish we could undo. Take text messages, for example. Once you click Send, there's no getting it back, so you have to be really careful what you say. I travel sometimes for work, but Amy and I keep in constant touch by texting. Because we're married—and *only* because we're married (Heb. 13:4)—sometimes we like to throw in a little Song of Solomon love action, if you know what I'm saying. Some "hot text."

One evening, she had texted me about our going for a walk in a vineyard together or something saucy like that, so when I got back to my room at about eleven o'clock, I texted her back how much I love her dental appeal: "Your teeth are like a flock of sheep coming up from the washing. Each has its twin, not one of them is missing." Only it was kind of racier than that. Okay, kind of *a lot* racier. Maybe even something about her fawns. (If you've never read Song of Solomon, you don't know what you're missing.)

Unfortunately, almost as soon as I hit Send, I noticed that I hadn't replied to the right conversation. I had two open conversations with Amy: our private one and a group text from earlier in the day. I had just sexted my wife's friends.

Have you ever seen that commercial where the guy accidentally sends an angry email to All, then he screams and drives all over, destroying everybody's computers? I know exactly how that dude felt. If I had the superpower of teleportation, I would have snatched every one of my wife's friends' phones and thrown them in the toilet. Unfortunately, I don't have any such powers. So there I was in full panic mode, staring at my phone, when it rang and nearly gave me a heart attack. Guess who it was? I tried to play it cool.

"Oh hi, baby. I was just thinking about you."

Amy sort of scream-whispered, "Do you *realize?*"

"Yes, I do!"

You will never find out what that text message said, because over the next few weeks, we had dinners with each of those couples in nice restaurants, and we paid for their meals to bribe them to secrecy.

You cannot unsend. But you can repent.

Some of you are going to come to the horrible realization that you can't unsleep with that person you slept with. But you can repent. You can't undo that dishonest financial deal you did. But you can repent. You can't unlook at what you looked at. But you can repent. You can't uncheat on your taxes, but you can repent. I'm not talking about some bad feeling you had because you got caught. I'm talking about a deep internal conviction, followed by immediate action.

You can repent.

As we'll see, Samson finally remembered who he was born to be. God didn't create him to entertain his enemies; he made him to fight for a higher purpose. He made him to fight for something eternally significant. Just like you. God created you to honor him and to glorify him with your life. He sent his Son to die for you, to model what it means to be a true warrior and not just an ego-driven wannabe hero.

Don't fall for the lure that your spiritual enemy dangles before you:

"Don't you wish you had just …?"
"Things would be different if only you'd …"
"Don't you wish you had the courage to risk making a
    change?"

Could have, would have, should have. You didn't. But remorse alone never changes anything. It's only repentance that says, "I'm not going to let what I did before stop me from doing what God wants me to do now. I'm turning away from my sin, and I'm turning toward God." You cannot change your past, but you can change your future.

Don't internalize the failure.

You are not what you did; you are who God says you are.

After all that he's been through, Samson finally realizes this truth. "When they stood him among the pillars, Samson said to the servant who held his hand, 'Put me where I can feel the pillars that support the temple, so that I may lean against them.' Now the temple was crowded with men and women; all the rulers of the Philistines were there, and on the roof were about three thousand men and women watching Samson perform. Then Samson prayed to the LORD, 'Sovereign LORD, remember me. Please, God, strengthen me just once more'" (Judg. 16:25–28).

Grab hold of this: we are Samson — you and me and millions of warriors around the world. No matter how many times we've blown it, we don't need a thousand more chances. We need only one. "Please, God, strengthen me just once more."

Samson's strength was never in his hair; his hair didn't have some kind of magical power. Samson told Delilah that if his hair was cut, his strength would leave him. But his strength came from God, not from his hair. Samson didn't seem to understand this distinction: his hair was not the source of his strength; his hair was just the symbol of whom he belonged to, the God to whom he had made his Nazirite vow. When Samson lost his hair, he lost his identity as God's anointed.

When Samson finally remembered whose he was and surrendered his self-reliance, he stepped across a spiritual line. Samson had always made everything about himself: the women, the feats of strength, taunting his enemies. But as he had done following an earlier victory, Samson decided to acknowledge God as the hero, rather than himself. "My God is the main character of this story. I will use everything I have and all that I am to bring him honor. Just once more."

In Samson's humiliated condition, no one recognized him as a threat. And that's exactly why he was a threat. No one believed there was anything good in him. But then he emptied everything that was left of himself and shared a private moment with God, just as you might want to do.

Maybe no one thinks you can make a difference, but they have no idea what God is doing in you at this moment. Some don't think you have any fight left in you, but they can't see the spiritual strength God is imparting to you. Others think you'll always wallow in your weaknesses, but they don't know that Christ's strength is alive in the middle of your mistakes. You might be down. But you are not out. You are his warrior.

Like Samson, you can pray, "Just once more, God. Please give me your strength, and I'll use the rest of my life to leverage everything that you've given me for your glory, your kingdom, and your name. Please give me one more chance."

Even in our failures God can accomplish his purposes. He really is *that* good.

Do you remember what God's purpose was for Samson's life? "He will take the lead in delivering Israel from the hands of the Philistines" (Judg. 13:5b). Now let's watch what happens in Judges 16:29–30: "Samson reached toward the two central pillars on which the temple stood. Bracing himself against them, his right hand on the one and his left hand on the other, Samson said, 'Let me die with the Philistines!' Then he pushed with all his might, and down came the temple on the rulers and all the people in it. Thus he killed many more when he died than while he lived."

These were the Philistine *rulers*—three thousand of them. All killed in one day. The Philistines he had killed for their clothes were just regular guys off the street. The thousand he killed with the donkey's jawbone were soldiers who were out looking for him. But these three thousand were the leaders of the enemy nation who had been oppressing his people for forty years. With just one last push, he fulfilled his purpose: taking "the lead in delivering Israel from the hands of the Philistines."

So no matter what you have done, God is not finished with you yet. Ask him for just one more chance. And God might do more through you in the next chapter of your life than in all of the previous ones combined.

5.6

PILLAR TALK

Even in the midst of your failures, God can still use you. No matter how many times you've messed up, if you're not dead, you're not done. There's more in you.

But Craig, you don't know all the stuff I did. I made so many mistakes. That just adds new dimensions of redemption to your story.

Once you're free, imagine kicking off any of these conversations:

But God!

"For years, I was a compulsive liar, but then God ..."

"For years, I was strung out on drugs, but then God ..."

"For years, I was addicted to pornography, but then
    God ..."

"For years, I was lukewarm in my faith, but then
    God ..."

"For years, I mismanaged money, but then God ..."

"For years, I didn't lead my family anywhere, but then
    God ..."

Understand this: Your victory gives other men hope. It gives them a vision for what could be. It holds out a hope that they too can escape from their darkness into his light. If Samson did it, you can do it. And if you can do it, others can do it. Best of all, you get to share how God made it happen in your life.

God isn't finished with you. You're not finished with you either. Do you have some pillars in your life that you need to push down? Pillars that are holding up what's been ruling you, oppressing you, tormenting you? What are they? Give every pillar a name. Is one of your pillars pride? Confess your weakness: "I need help. I'm alone. I'm afraid. I feel like a failure. I've been doing something I wish I wasn't doing, but I don't know how to stop. I'm addicted. I've been lying. I'm not who people think I am." Push down that pillar of pride.

Is one of your pillars anger? Acknowledge your condition: "I'm mad at the whole world. But I'm mad at myself too. Why can't my life be how I want it to be?" Push down that pillar of anger.

Is one of your pillars lust? Express your vulnerability: "I just can't stop myself. I don't want to look, but I do. I wish I could be free, but I can't seem to escape the urges that overtake me." Push down that pillar of lust.

And don't just think about what your pillars are. Take action. You need to write them down. Let me tell you why. One evening I went to the grocery store to get frozen fruit for smoothies. Because it was such a simple errand, I didn't bother making a list. When I got home an hour later with two hundred dollars' worth of food, none of it was frozen fruit. Why? Because I'm a man, and men need to write things down to get them done.

Now grab a piece of paper and something to write with. Write down your pillars. Leave some space next to each one to write how you're going to push it down. Don't overcomplicate this. Keep it simple.

If you want different results, you have to *do* something different.

his is where the rubber meets the road. Call to get counseling. Check yourself in for rehab. Confess to godly men in your life — and to your wife. Confess to your small group. If you don't have a small group, get one. Get help managing your money. Go to a financial counselor. Find a mentor who has a career you admire.

Stop skipping church whenever you feel like it because you stayed up late the night before or there's a game on or you want to go to the lake or for whatever other reason you want to make up. Stop being a phony. Wholeheartedly commit your life to Christ. Stop just going to church and consuming. Get yourself and your family involved. Make a difference. Serve. Tithe. Give offerings. Pray. Engage in the life of the church. Grow spiritually.

Stop pretending. Do something different. Act.

Stop griping that your marriage is bad. Start loving your way to an amazing marriage. Lead your way into a God-centered marriage with the wife you already have. Every day, recount all the reasons you fell in love with her in the first place. Start really looking at her again and noticing how amazing she is. Then tell her. Pursue her again like you did when you first met.

Don't go another day without spending time with your kids. Get over yourself and your idea of how much money you think you have to make. Stop spending so much and scale back your lifestyle. Play with your kids. Tell them stories. Ride bikes with them. Hang out with them. Read them books and don't skip pages. Listen to them. Laugh with them. Pray with them every night before bed and every morning before school — and whenever else they want. This won't wait. Blink and they'll be gone and you will have missed your chance.

If you're not married but you want to be, go get a nice haircut from a real stylist. Sell your game console and use the time you would have spent gaming doing things that will make you worth some godly girl's time: studying God's Word, learning be a man of God, getting yourself in spiritual shape. Get into a men's group with guys who will hold you accountable to a biblical standard of morality, guys who will help you mold yourself into the male version of the godly woman you've always hoped for. Shower regularly. Brush your teeth. Use mouthwash and hair product. Get out of your house and actually talk to people. Put yourself out there. When you meet a girl, pray with her. Open the door for her. Write her notes. And keep your paws off her body until you've walked her down the aisle.

Don't settle for remorse. Once you identify a pillar, don't carve your initials into it. Push it down. Then turn and walk away from the rubble. Turn away from your sin, and turn toward God. Do something different from what you've been doing. You have a calling on your life. Find it. Then give everything you have to pursue it. "Though the righteous fall seven times, they rise again" (Prov. 24:16).

Now is the time to stop flirting around with God. Stop kicking the spiritual tires and lying to yourself that one day you might really seek him. Today is that day. It's time to call on Jesus. Ask him to save you. Trust your whole life to him. He's there. He's here. He's waiting. Give your life to him. Do it now.

If you're a Christian, you have resurrection power within you. Don't give up. Don't try just to "be a stronger man." Satan loves making strong men weak. God loves making weak men strong. Don't try just to "be a better man." Be God's man. Stop trying to tell your story. Start telling his. It's not about you. It's about him. Push those pillars down. Die to yourself so you can live for him.

THE WARRIOR'S PRAYER

What Samson did at the end was right, but it also was easy. What he did was dramatic, but it was easy. You read that correctly. I believe it's actually easy for a man to give up his life. Every one of us has a hero inside who's ready to do that.

Don't believe me? Picture this: some thug breaks into your house in the middle of the night and puts someone you love in danger. What do you do? Dive out a window? No! You leap out of bed in your boxers, you grab a lamp or whatever's close, and you beat his brains out with it. You're going to stop that sucker, or you're going to die trying. You wouldn't hesitate. You'd give your life for someone you love.

Giving your life one time is easy. You know what's hard? Giving your life daily. Paul said, "I die every day" (1 Cor. 15:31 NIV 1984). Real men give their lives *daily*. The world has yet to see what God will do through one man whose heart is surrendered to him.

I know you may feel like you've disqualified yourself from that opportunity. I know the feeling.

Do you think Satan doesn't tell me that all the time? "Who

do you think you are calling yourself a pastor with your jacked-up self? You chased down teenage boys for giving you the finger. With your kids in the car. You tell inappropriate jokes like you're a middle school boy — *in your Christian book about Samson.* You dirty-texted your wife's Bible study group, for goodness' sake."

Remorse rolls in regret like a pig wallows in mud.

"I shouldn't have ..."

"I didn't ..."

"I wish I had ..."

But that doesn't change anything. That's not what you're going to do. Not anymore. Even after everything you've done — no matter how terrible, how scary, how secretive, how offensive — your Father wants to forgive you. He loves you. He made you to have a warrior's heart just like his. If you're serious about fighting the right fight, then you must depend on him.

Would you dare to pray this prayer with me?

God, I'm so sorry. I've been living my life for myself. I made everything about me. I've been trying to be the hero of my own story. I've been squandering the gifts you gave me. Even when I have used your gifts, I've tried to use them for selfish gain. That was my choice and my fault. I accept the responsibility for all that I've done.

And I repent, God. Please forgive me. You promised in your Word that if I confess my sins, you'll be faithful and just, you'll forgive me of my sins, and you'll cleanse me from my unrighteousness. Remember me, God. Show me all of the pillars in my life, the things that have been keeping me from being your man. Then please give me the strength to push them down.

My life isn't about me anymore. I surrender my heart to you,

Lord. I want to be your man, telling your story. Your Word says that you adopted me as your son. Thank you that I am not what I have done but that I am who you say I am. Please make my outward life show other people that I'm your man.

Father, teach me how to live my life in a way that pleases you, that brings you the glory that only you deserve. Show me how to be the man you created me to be. I am your man. Show this world what you will do through me. Here I am, Lord. Send me. Use my life as you see fit. Show me what battles to fight. I am your man. Thank you so much for all the ways you're going to use me to accomplish your purposes in this world. Thank you for making me a warrior. In Jesus' name, amen.

If you'll pray that prayer and mean it, I can promise you that the act of faith that brought about the end of Samson's life can become, through Christ, the beginning of your new life.

You don't have to hit rock bottom to bring down the pillars of pride, lust, and entitlement. You don't have to pretend to be stronger than you are. You only have to be the man God made you to be. His beloved son.

His warrior.

ACKNOWLEDGMENTS

Thank you to all my friends for your help with this book. It wouldn't be close to what it is without you all.

I'm especially grateful for:

Dudley Delffs: You are a warrior with words. Thanks for having my back. I've always got yours.

Tom Dean, Tracy Danz, Brian Phipps, John Raymond, and the whole team at Zondervan: I'm honored to work with you all.

Brannon Golden: You are the editing ninja.

Tom Winters: Thanks for "fighting" for the men's book.

Lori Tapp: Thanks for being a local rock star.

Pastor Steven Furtick, Brandon Donaldson, Adrianne Manning: Thanks for your valuable feedback and suggestions. You made a big difference.

Catie, Mandy, Anna, Sam, Stephen, Joy: No dad is more proud of his kids than I am of you!

Amy: You are the love of my life. Let's grow old together.

Fight: A DVD Study

Winning the Battles That Matter Most

Craig Groeschel

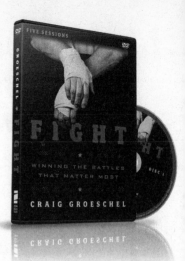

Author and pastor Craig Groeschel helps you uncover who you really are — a man created in the image of God with a warrior's heart — and how to fight the good fight for what's right. You will find the strength to fight the battles you know you need to fight — the ones that determine the state of your heart, the quality of your marriage, and the spiritual health of your family. The battles that make you dependent on God as the source of your strength. The battles that make you come alive.

Craig looks at the life of Samson, showing how much we have in common with this guy. Things didn't work out so well for him in the end. But by looking at his life, you'll learn how to defeat the demons that make strong men weak. You'll become who God made you to be:

A man who knows how to fight for what's right.

You have the heart of a warrior.

Learn how to fight with faith, with prayer, and with the Word of God. Then, when your enemy begin attacks, fight for the righteous cause that God gave you. Draw a line in the sand. Make your enemy pay. Make sure he gets the message. Don't cross a warrior. Don't mess with this man of God. Come out fighting.

And don't show up for this fight unarmed.

Use the weapons God gave you, and you'll win. Can you feel it? It's inside you.

It's time to fight like a man.

Fight Study Guide

Winning the Battles That Matter Most

Craig Groeschel

In *Fight*, a five-session, video-based small group Bible study, pastor and bestselling author Craig Groeschel explores the life of Samson, helping you uncover who you really are – a man created with a warrior's heart in the image of God – and how to stand up and fight for what's right.

Find the strength to fight the battles you know you need to fight – the ones that determine the state of your heart, the quality of your marriage, and the spiritual health of your family. The battles that make you dependent on God as the source of your strength. The battles that make you come alive.

Craig looks at the life of Samson, showing how much we have in common with this guy. Things didn't work out so well for him in the end. But by looking at his life, you'll learn how to defeat the demons that make strong men weak. You'll become who God made you to be – a man who knows how to fight for what's right.

Learn how to fight with faith, with prayer, and with the Word of God. Then, when your enemy begin attacks, fight for the righteous cause that God gave you. Draw a line in the sand. Make your enemy pay. Make sure he gets the message. Don't cross a warrior. Don't mess with this man of God. Come out fighting.

And don't show up for this fight unarmed.

Use the weapons God gave you, and you'll win. Can you feel it? It's inside you.

It's time to fight like a man.

Designed for use with the *Fight* DVD (sold separately).

Altar Ego

Becoming Who God Says You Are

Craig Groeschel

You are not who you think you are. In fact, according to bestselling author Craig Groeschel, you need to take your idea of your own identity, lay it down on the altar, and sacrifice it. Give it to God. Offer it up.

Why? Because you are who God says you are. And until you've sacrificed your broken concept of your identity, you won't become who you are meant to be.

When we place our false labels and self-deception on the altar of God's truth, we discover who we really are as his sons and daughters. Instead of an outward-driven, approval-based ego, we learn to live with an "altar ego," God's vision of who we are becoming.

Discover how to trade in your broken ego and unleash your altar ego to become a living sacrifice. Once we know our true identity and are growing in Christlike character, then we can behave accordingly, with bold behavior, bold prayers, bold words, and bold obedience.

Altar Ego reveals who God says you are, and then calls you to live up to it.

Small Group Curriculum Also Available:
• 5-Session DVD – 9780310894933
• Study Guide – 9780310894940
• Study Guide with DVD – 9780310693031

Available in stores and online!

Soul Detox

Clean Living in a Contaminated World

Craig Groeschel

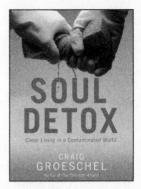

As standards of conduct continue to erode in our shock-proof world, we must fight the soul pollution threatening our health, our faith, and our witness to others. Without even knowing it, people willingly inhale secondhand toxins, poisoning their relationship with God and stunting their spiritual growth.

Soul Detox examines the toxins that assault us daily, including toxic influences, toxic emotions, and toxic behaviors.

By examining the toxins that assault us daily, this book offers the ultimate spiritual intervention with ways to remain clean, pure, and focused on the standard of God's holiness.

Small Group Curriculum Also Available:
- 5-Session DVD – 9780310894919
- Study Guide – 9780310687528
- Study Guide with DVD – 9780310685760

Weird

Because Normal Isn't Working

Craig Groeschel,
author of The Christian Atheist

Normal people are stressed, overwhelmed, and exhausted. Many of their relationships are, at best, strained and, in most cases, just surviving. Even though we live in one of the most prosperous places on earth, normal is still living paycheck to paycheck and never getting ahead. In our oversexed world, lust, premarital sex, guilt, and shame are far more common than purity, virginity, and a healthy married sex life. And when it comes to God, the majority believe in him, but the teachings of Scripture rarely make it into their everyday lives.

Simply put, normal isn't working.

Groeschel's "weird" views will help you break free from the norm to lead a radically abnormal (and endlessly more fulfilling) life.

Small Group Curriculum Also Available:
- 6-Session DVD – 9780310894971
- Study Guide – 9780310894986
- Study Guide with DVD – 9780310684305

The Christian Atheist

Believing in God but Living as If He Doesn't Exist

Craig Groeschel

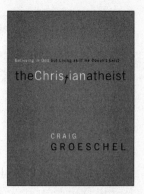

"The more I looked, the more I found Christian Atheists everywhere."

Former Christian Atheist Craig Groeschel knows his subject all too well. After over a decade of successful ministry, he had to make a painful admission: although he believed in God, he was leading his church as if God doesn't exist.

To Christians and non-Christians alike, to the churched and the unchurched, the journey leading up to Groeschel's admission and the journey that follows—from his family and his upbringing to the lackluster and even diametrically opposed expressions of faith he encountered—will look and sound like the story of their own lives.

Groeschel's personal journey toward a more authentic God-honoring life is more relevant than ever.

Christians and Christian Atheists everywhere will be nodding their heads as they are challenged to honestly ask, Am I putting my whole faith in God but still living as if everything were up to me?

Small Group Curriculum Also Available:
- 6-Session DVD – 9780310329794
- Study Guide – 9780310329756
- Study Guide with DVD – 9780310494300

Available in stores and online!

ZONDERVAN®
.com

It Book with DVD

How Churches and Leaders Can Get It and Keep It

Craig Groeschel

Pack containing one book and one DVD. When Craig Groeschel founded LifeChurch. tv, the congregation met in a borrowed two-car garage, with ratty furnishings and faulty audiovisual equipment. But people were drawn there, sensing a powerful, life-changing force Groeschel calls "It." What is It, and how can you and your ministry get—and keep—It? Combining in-your-face honesty with off-the-wall humor, this book tells how any believer can obtain It, get It back, and guard It. One of today's most innovative church leaders, Groeschel provides profile interviews with Mark Driscoll, Perry Noble, Tim Stevens, Mark Batterson, Jud Wilhite, and Dino Rizzo. This lively book and DVD will challenge churches and their leaders to maintain the spiritual balance that results in experiencing It in their lives.

What Is God Really Like?

Craig Groeschel, General Editor

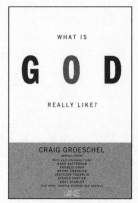

For the past two years, Craig Groeschel
(www.lifechurch.tv) and his church have
hosted an international multichurch campaign called One Prayer, a monthlong con-
certed focus on unifying the many different,
diverse churches participating by praying together and serving their local communities.

In 2009, the One Prayer campaign attracted more than 2,000
churches and more than 1,000,000 church members. Many of these
churches are high-profile evangelical churches with pastors who are
also successful authors and speakers. The campaign continues to at-
tract interest from more and more churches and ministries. The 2010
campaign, scheduled for June, is expected to grow by 50 percent.

This compilation book features chapters by seventeen passionate church leaders, including Andy Stanley, Francis Chan, Jentezen
Franklin, Perry Noble, Steven Furtick, and others.

Available in stores and online!

Share Your Thoughts

With the Author: Your comments will be forwarded to the author when you send them to *zauthor@zondervan.com*.

With Zondervan: Submit your review of this book by writing to *zreview@zondervan.com*.

Free Online Resources at
www.zondervan.com

Daily Bible Verses and Devotions: Enrich your life with daily Bible verses or devotions that help you start every morning focused on God. Visit www.zondervan.com/newsletters.

Free Email Publications: Sign up for newsletters on Christian living, academic resources, church ministry, fiction, children's resources, and more. Visit www.zondervan.com/newsletters.

Zondervan Bible Search: Find and compare Bible passages in a variety of translations at www.zondervanbiblesearch.com.

Other Benefits: Register to receive online benefits like coupons and special offers, or to participate in research.